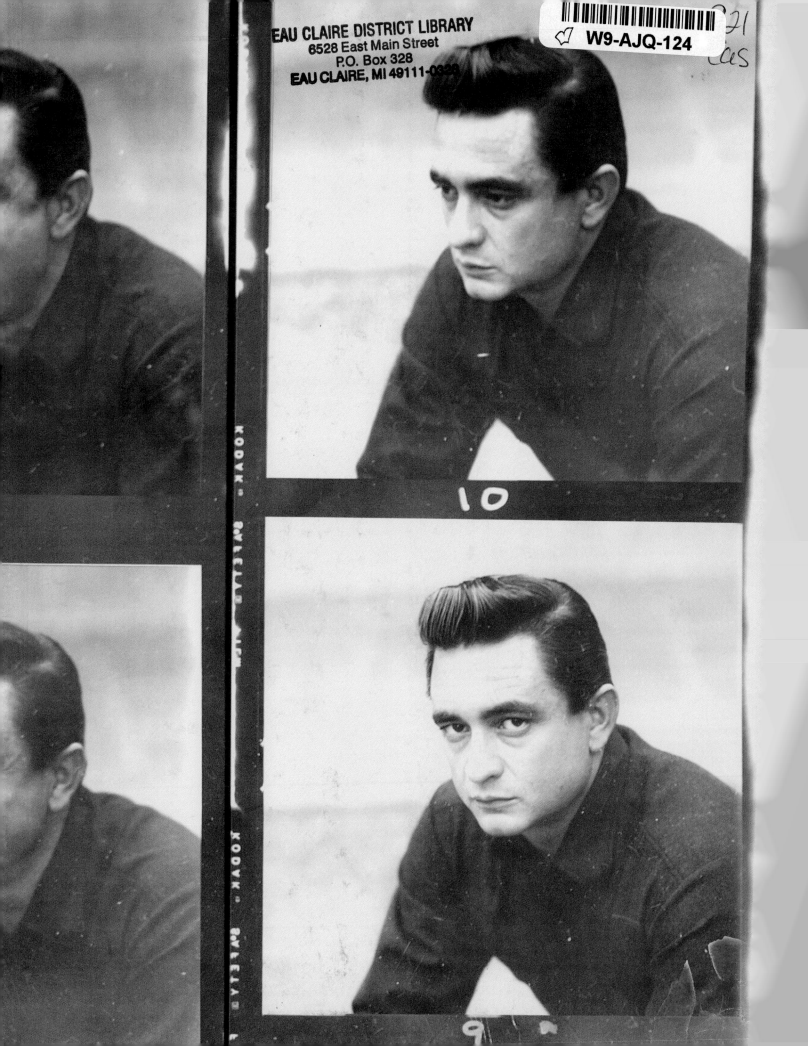

CASH
AN AMERICAN MAN

By
Bill Miller

Edited by
Mark Vancil and Jacob Hoye

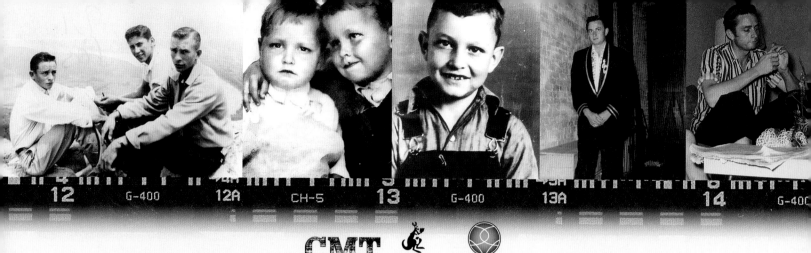

POCKET BOOKS, a division of Simon & Schuster, Inc.
1230 Avenue of the Americas, New York, NY 10020
CMT © 2004 Country Music Television, Inc.,
a division of MTV Networks, a Viacom company.

Text and other materials copyright © 2004 by Bill Miller
Compilation copyright © 2004 by Rare Air Ltd.
Cash Interview with Kurt Loder ©2004 by MTV Networks,
a division of Viacom International, Inc.

Library of Congress Cataloging-in-Publication Data is available upon request.

ISBN: 0-7434-9629-9(HC)
0-7434-9950-6(PBK)

First Pocket Books hardcover edition May 2004

10 9 8 7 6 5 4 3 2 1

POCKET and colophon are registered trademarks of Simon & Schuster, Inc.

Designed by Rare Air Media

Visit us on the World Wide Web

www.simonsays.com
www.cmt.com
www.rareairmedia.com

For information regarding special discounts for bulk purchases, please contact Simon & Schuster Special Sales
at 1-800-456-6798 or business@simonandschuster.com

Photo & Art Credits

Photography except noted below © Bill Miller Collection

ABC publicity photo	4, 69, 134, 135, 145		Alan Messer	121
American Recordings publicity photo	76, 155		Bill Miller	4, 14, 167
American Recordings	154		Michael Rougier/Stringe,	
Mike Coffey	81		Time Life pictures, Getty Images	60
Columbia publicity photo	4, 5, 72, 167		Lamar Sorrento	25, 146-147
Columbia Records	8, 53, 131		Unknown	37, 50, 58, 69, 92, 127, 164, 165
Dan Gillotte	173		Barrie Wetzell	168
Mike Maas	49		White House photo	128, 129
Jim Marshall	8, 70		Ray Witherell	167
Mike Maxwell	107			

Acknowledgements

DEDICATION | *For my best friend, partner, lover and soul mate, Shannon — I love you. For Billy, Blake and Jordan — you are the light of my life.*

I would like to acknowledge the following people, in no particular order, for their contributions to my life, my collection and more.

To my mom and dad, for indulging me as I relentlessly pursued my interest in Johnny Cash. Without their support, I don't know that any of this would have been possible. To Lou Robin, Johnny's longtime manager, and his wife, Karen, for the incredible kindness and friendship they have granted me for 30-plus years. To Kathy Cash, my surrogate sister, for her loving friendship and support, and for trusting me to preserve and protect her dad's legacy. To Cindy Cash, my friend, for the same reasons. To Irene Gibbs, for many years of valued friendship and guidance. To Reba Hancock, for the kindness and generosity she has shown me since I was a kid. To Kelly Hancock, for years of loyalty to Johnny and friendship to me. To Karen Adams, my new friend, who I regret not getting to know better years ago. To John Carter Cash, for his support of this project. To Bob Sullivan, for his

assistance in making this book a reality. To Peter Lewry, author of *I've Been Everywhere: A Johnny Cash Chronicle,* for aiding me in recalling the dates of events over 30 years. To John L. Smith, whose incredible discography of Johnny's work proved to be an invaluable resource for me. To Mark Vancil, for his support and enthusiasm in allowing this to be my story. And to Johnny Cash, for contributing so many wonderful pieces to my collection and supporting my quest to build an archive that will chronicle his life in a meaningful way. Most of all, John, thanks for the memories.

There are countless other precious folks who worked for and with Johnny that I would like to thank for enriching my life along the way. You know who you are, and you know how I feel.

— Bill Miller

This journey around the corners of Johnny Cash's life took on the wonder of the man himself, thanks to all those who came along. Bill and Shannon Miller turned out to be the kind of exceptional people one would expect to be found inside Johnny's inner circle. At MTV, Jacob Hoye and Walter Einenkel made every meeting and every phone call a joy, a rare occurrence indeed. There is a spirit that runs through them and flowed on through this book as well. At Pocket Books, Scott Shannon and Ed Schlesinger made all of us feel as if we were creating something larger than ourselves. In all moments, they were professional, kind and caring

beyond any expectation. Ken Leiker did his usual masterful job seeking out the opportunity and refining the text, and Nick DeCarlo and John Vieceli turned thousands of words and images into a wonderful book, despite months of long hours. Their innate goodness and talents can be found on every page of this book. And at home, as always, the best of me comes from the wonder of Laura, Alexandra, Samantha, Isabella and my boy, Jonah.

— Mark Vancil

Special contributor: Kurt Loder

Special thanks: Walter Einenkel

Many thanks: Brian Philips, Janet Rollé, Liate Stehlik, Louise Burke, Raquel Bruno, Aaron Cummins, Erica Laden, David Saslow, Heather Stas, J.P. Jones, Wenonah and Lucas, WBOB, and Rockpants.

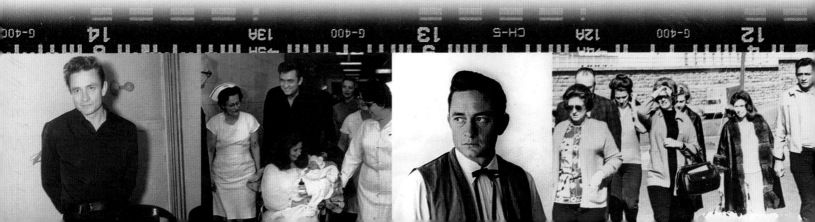

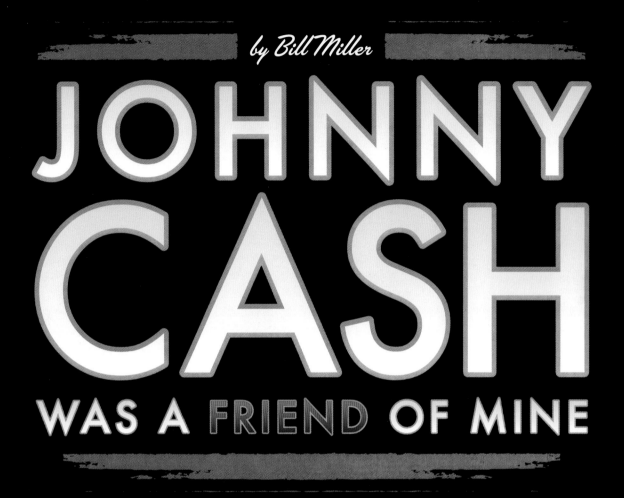

by *Bill Miller*

JOHNNY CASH

WAS A FRIEND OF MINE

ACTUALLY, HE WAS MUCH MORE THAN A FRIEND.

HE WAS MY HERO, MY MENTOR, THE GODFATHER OF MY YOUNGEST SON

AND AN INSPIRATION TO ME EVERY DAY OF MY LIFE

SINCE I WAS 9 YEARS OLD.

YOU HAVE PROBABLY SEEN, HEARD OR READ ONE OF THE HUNDREDS OF TRIBUTES FROM ARTISTS ACROSS VIRTUALLY EVERY MUSIC GENRE TO U.S. PRESIDENTS TO FRIENDS WHO HAD A PERSONAL AFFINITY FOR JOHNNY CASH. HIS CAREER ACHIEVEMENTS HAVE BEEN RECOUNTED THOUSANDS OF TIMES IN EVERY MEDIUM. THIS BOOK IS ABOUT THE MAN BEHIND THE HITS, THE GENTLE SOUL WHO TOUCHED MILLIONS AROUND THE GLOBE, AND THE PURITY OF SPIRIT THAT FUELED IT ALL. HE WAS A MAN OF LEGENDARY INTEGRITY, INCREDIBLE TALENT AND A DEPTH OF SPIRIT THAT WILL LIVE FOREVER IN HIS MUSIC. HE WAS, IN MANY WAYS, THE QUINTESSENTIAL AMERICAN MAN.

It is about the Johnny Cash I was privileged to know and love for more than 34 years. In words and images, I have tried to lift the curtain on an amazing man and his life through an intimate collection of memories that Johnny helped compile. For more than three decades, Johnny and I put together a collection that covers just about every facet of his life. From the handwritten lyrics to the personal notes he wrote to those he held closest, this book is an attempt to reveal the wonder of a man who became an icon.

I first discovered the magic in 1969. A girl in my third-grade class brought his album, *Johnny Cash at Folsom Prison*, to school for show-and-tell. Our teacher had no idea who Johnny was, but she found out quickly from the opening, electrifying pronouncement on the album: "Hello, I'm Johnny Cash." I had never heard any music like it. In my house, in a small town more than an hour from Palm Springs, California, my connection to music had come through my parents and older brother. My mother and father spun Bing Crosby

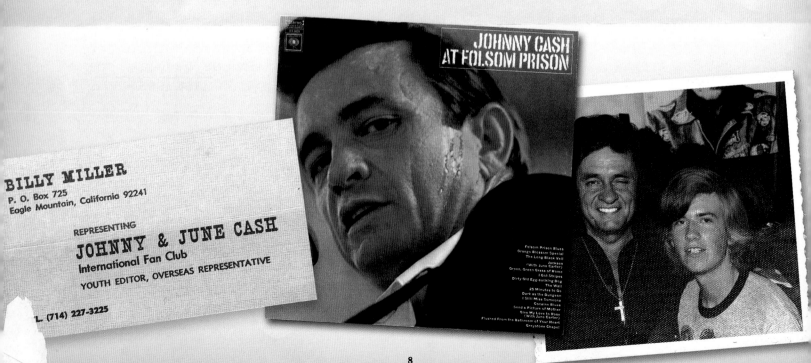

records, and my brother played the songs of Jimi Hendrix and Jim Morrison. I didn't care much for music—until I heard Johnny Cash.

That third-grade experience led to a lifetime interest that grew into a long-lasting friendship. I bought every Johnny Cash album when it came out. I collected every magazine and poster featuring Johnny that I could find. I saw every movie that Johnny was in and all of his television appearances. I joined the Johnny Cash fan club and within a year became the Youth Editor for a series of journals published by the club.

vantage point, the band members looked like ants. Eventually I walked down through the crowd and toward the stage.

Johnny was singing "Orange Blossom Special," a song in which he used two harmonicas for the instrumental bridge, as I reached the front of the stage. I raised my Kodak Hawkeye Instamatic camera, and as I looked at the huge, awesome man above me, he made eye contact and tossed me one of the harmonicas (pages 30–31). I froze as the harmonica came my way, but quickly scrambled to the floor to retrieve it. When Johnny finished his last encore, I dashed off to the lobby, hoping to

As I grew older, I attended hundreds of Johnny's concerts. Early on, I met Lou Robin, Johnny's manager, who took a liking to the kid he and Johnny called "Little Billy Miller." The first few times Lou allowed me to go backstage and meet the great man, I just sat and stared at Johnny. I was too much in awe to speak. For his part, Johnny was more gracious and wonderful than a little boy had any right to expect.

In 1973, I found out the Johnny Cash Show was coming to Denver, Colorado, about five hours from my family's home in New Mexico. By the time I got up the nerve to ask my dad if he'd take me to the show, the only seats available in Denver Auditorium Arena were those far from the stage. From my

meet him. Seconds later, Johnny, escorted by six police officers, strode through the lobby. I was amazed at how big he looked and mesmerized by his swinging arms and long strides. I ran ahead and turned and faced him. Johnny paused and took my outreached hand. "Hi son," he said, "how ya doin'?" With that, he slipped into a black limousine and disappeared into the chilly darkness. That was my first Johnny Cash concert. My life would never be the same again.

As I became a regular at Johnny's concerts and got to know him, he welcomed me into his inner circle. I was always made to feel at home, not only by Johnny but also by other members of his concert troupe and his business associates and family. Johnny surrounded himself with people who had many of his qualities: kindness, consideration, respect and a down-to-earth nature.

What always struck me about Johnny was how he treated everyone equally. It didn't matter whether it was a Hollywood celebrity or a country boy asking for an autograph, Johnny took an interest in whoever was standing before him. He would ask the names of people's children and graciously look at family photos that fans brought to show him. Humble and sincere, he had a gift for making every person feel like they mattered. He was human to a fault, pure and simple in the way a child is.

Johnny went out of his way to touch the common man. There are hundreds of stories about him reaching out to the downtrodden and less fortunate. And who knows how many other good deeds he performed that went unnoticed, for Johnny never called attention to his charitable works. Maybe it was Johnny's poor childhood that made him feel a kinship with the less fortunate. From my experiences with him, I know this for certain: He liked people. Perhaps he drew some

JOHNNY CASH

RE: GUILD Guitar   Hendersonville Tn.
Model D60SBE   Feb. 23 1993
S.N. D600067

Mr. Bill Miller.

Dear Bill,
    Please accept this guitar of mine as a personal gift and token of my friendship.
    I've used this guitar on every concert for ~~more~~ more than 10 years.
    It plays better than ever. I hope you enjoy it.
                    Best Wishes,
                    your Friend.
                    Johny Cash

Guild

JOHNNY CASH Hendersonville, TN
Feb 23, 1993

MASTER Jordan Cash Miller,

Welcome to the world. I hope
We can leave it in better shape
for you than you've found it now.
You're going to do good!
You come from good stock.
the World is your Apple.
Peel it.

Best Wishes,
Love,
Encouragement,
and Prayers,

Johnny Cash

measure of understanding about himself through the experiences of others. Contrary to his public badass, macho image, Johnny Cash was a sensitive, thoughtful and caring man.

Johnny was a collector with many interests. He collected autographs of U.S. presidents, signed books, Remington art and antique firearms, among many other items. He knew that I had a large collection of Johnny Cash material and respected my continuing efforts to add more items. On many occasions, I received packages from his Nashville, Tennessee, office with various treasures enclosed. I would call his personal assistant, Kelly Hancock, to inquire why I had received the items. Her explanation was always the same: "John said, 'This belongs with Bill Miller.'"

He sent guitars, harmonicas, handwritten lyrics, personal notes, letters, documents, original artwork and costumes. He was generous to a fault with me, although I never asked him for anything. I know he believed that all the

items he sent me would have a good home for years to come.

I couldn't begin to recount my memories of Johnny within the confines of this book. Our private conversations ranged from politics to collectibles to our kids to "a whole lot of nothing," as Johnny liked to say and which he enjoyed most. He didn't have to feel "on" around me, and I think that's why we felt comfortable around each other. I never asked him why he wore black, or if he had been in prison. (He never was, other than to perform.) We never talked about show business. He knew I had an immense appreciation and admiration for him, but it was never something that needed to be said. There was something about the man and his music that touched my soul. I felt it, and I believe Johnny knew it.

The last time I saw Johnny was in August 2003. He had some serious health problems and had been in and out of the hospital. My wife, Shannon, and I arrived at his home and spent an hour with him. We were amazed at how great he looked and how well he was doing. He was warm, funny and full of vitality. As we were getting

Top: **Bill** and his wife, Shannon, with **Johnny** in **August 2003**.
Bottom: **Bill's** sons Blake and Billy with **Johnny** in **August 1993**.

ready to leave, Johnny reached down beside his chair for a bag. Inside was a beautiful stained-glass item that featured a hand-painted portrait of Johnny, his late wife, June, and their son, John Carter Cash. The piece had hung in the window of John and June's kitchen for more than 30 years. Johnny said, "Hang this in your kitchen against the window, so the light shines through." Tears came to my eyes, and a smile came to Johnny's face. I said all there was left to say: "I love you."

Johnny had summoned every bit of strength he had to let me know that he was OK, that he would be OK. He had given Shannon and I a precious memento, something that meant a lot to him, knowing that it would mean a lot to us as well.

We were amazed at how good he looked that day. I had no idea it would be the last time we'd be together. But he knew. Less than three weeks later, he was gone.

As I pulled items from my collection to share with you on the pages that follow, I experienced a myriad of emotions: tears, laughter, happiness, sadness and, on occasion, numbness. Going through all these treasures allowed me to become a kid again. Many times, I relived the excitement I felt every time I saw Johnny.

THE LIGHT SHINES THROUGH THE STAINED-GLASS ORNAMENT THAT NOW HANGS

IN MY KITCHEN WINDOW. NO OTHER MAN HAS EVER MEANT AS MUCH TO ME

AS JOHNNY CASH. I MISS HIM IMMENSELY.

This was Johnny's home office, a small work space and retreat off the master bedroom that was off-limits to all but a few. Johnny spent much of the last few months of his life in this room. He kept trinkets and other items that had a lot of meaning to him in the office. The framed piece on his desk is an Abraham Lincoln document that I had given him as a gift.

Johnny served four years in the Air Force and attained the rank of sergeant while stationed in Germany. He served as a radio intercept operator and learned to type an impressive 150 words per minute. It was in Germany that Johnny formed his first band and music became a driving force in his life. He once joked, "I spent 20 years in the Air Force from 1950 to 1954." This is one of the uniforms Johnny wore during his stint.

THE TENNESSEE TWO

J ohnny returned to Memphis, Tennessee, in 1954 after being discharged from the Air Force. He was squeezing out a living as a door-to-door appliance salesman when he found out through his brother, Roy, about two men who were trying to organize a band. Marshall Grant and Luther Perkins worked in a Memphis auto repair shop. After hours, they picked guitars and sang for friends and coworkers, and Johnny soon joined them. Luther played lead guitar, and Marshall played an upright bass that he had bought used. Johnny knew three chords on his acoustic guitar. None of the three was an accomplished player, but the stark, raw and unadorned sound the three produced on their instruments was the ideal comple- ment to Johnny's strong, clear baritone voice. Johnny hoped the trio would become a gospel group, but Sun Records founder Sam Phillips discouraged that plan. After listening to the group, Phillips told Johnny, Marshall and Luther to come see him again when they had changed their repertoire. And that's exactly what they did.

Johnny's first single, "Cry! Cry! Cry!," was released on the Sun Records label in June 1955. "Hey Porter" was on the flip side, a song that became a Cash standard. "Cry! Cry! Cry!" made it to number 14 on the country charts on November 26, 1955, and fell off after a week. Johnny recorded "Folsom Prison Blues" prior to "Cry! Cry! Cry!," but Sun founder Sam Phillips thought the latter would have more commercial appeal.

Johnny was signed by Sun Records in 1954; these are his first publicity photos. Years later, Johnny and I were in Palm Springs, California, when talks began about a motion picture based on his life. His first choice for the lead role was Johnny Depp. I had these photos with me, and Johnny asked if he could have copies to send to Depp. "I think he looks like me when I was young," Johnny said.

Johnny didn't have much money when he got into the music business, so his mother, Carrie Cash (opposite page) made his early stage costumes. This pair of pants, sewn by Mrs. Cash, features multicolored lamé trim down each leg. Johnny often wore these pants in his early concerts, matching them with different jackets.

"MY MOTHER TOLD ME TO KEEP ON SINGING, AND THAT KEPT ME WORKING THROUGH THE COTTON FIELDS. SHE SAID, 'GOD HAS HIS HAND ON YOU. YOU'LL BE SINGING FOR THE WORLD SOMEDAY.'"

— JOHNNY CASH

Marty Stuart gave me this Lamar Sorrento painting of Johnny. Lamar is a well-known and highly respected artist, and he also leads a surf band. Lamar told me, "I've had a hard time painting Johnny, but I'm getting better." His whimsical style is what makes his work so compelling. Many celebrities, including Marty and members of the Rolling Stones, collect Lamar's work.

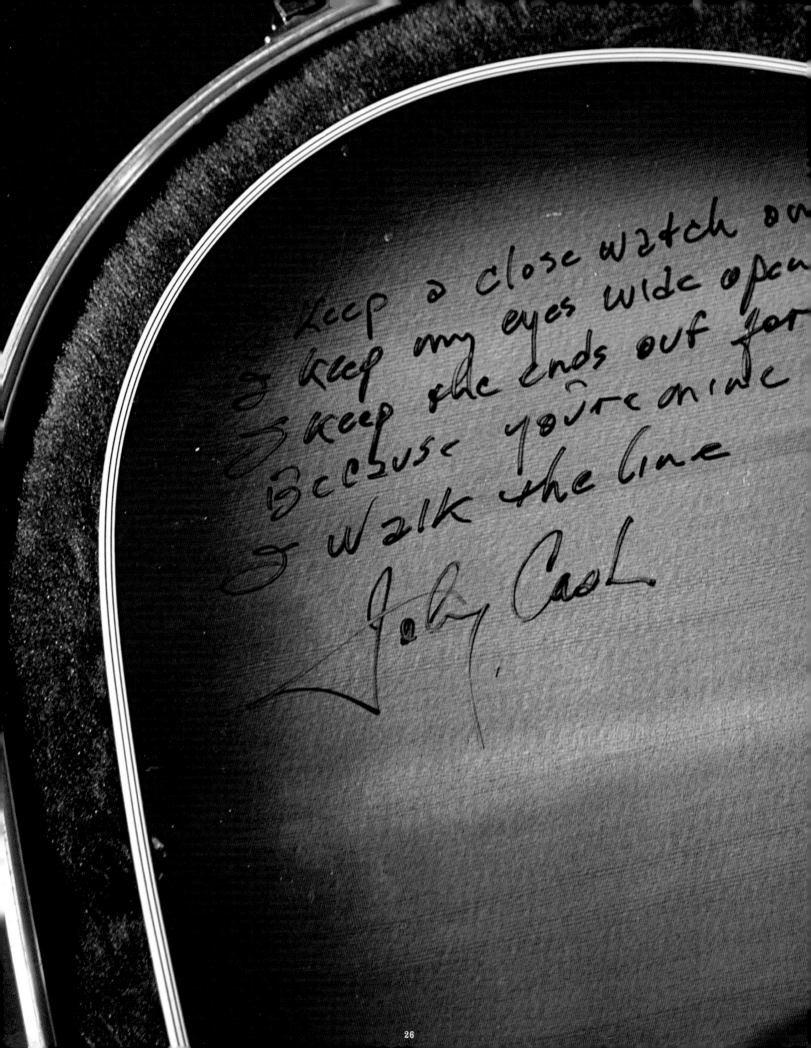

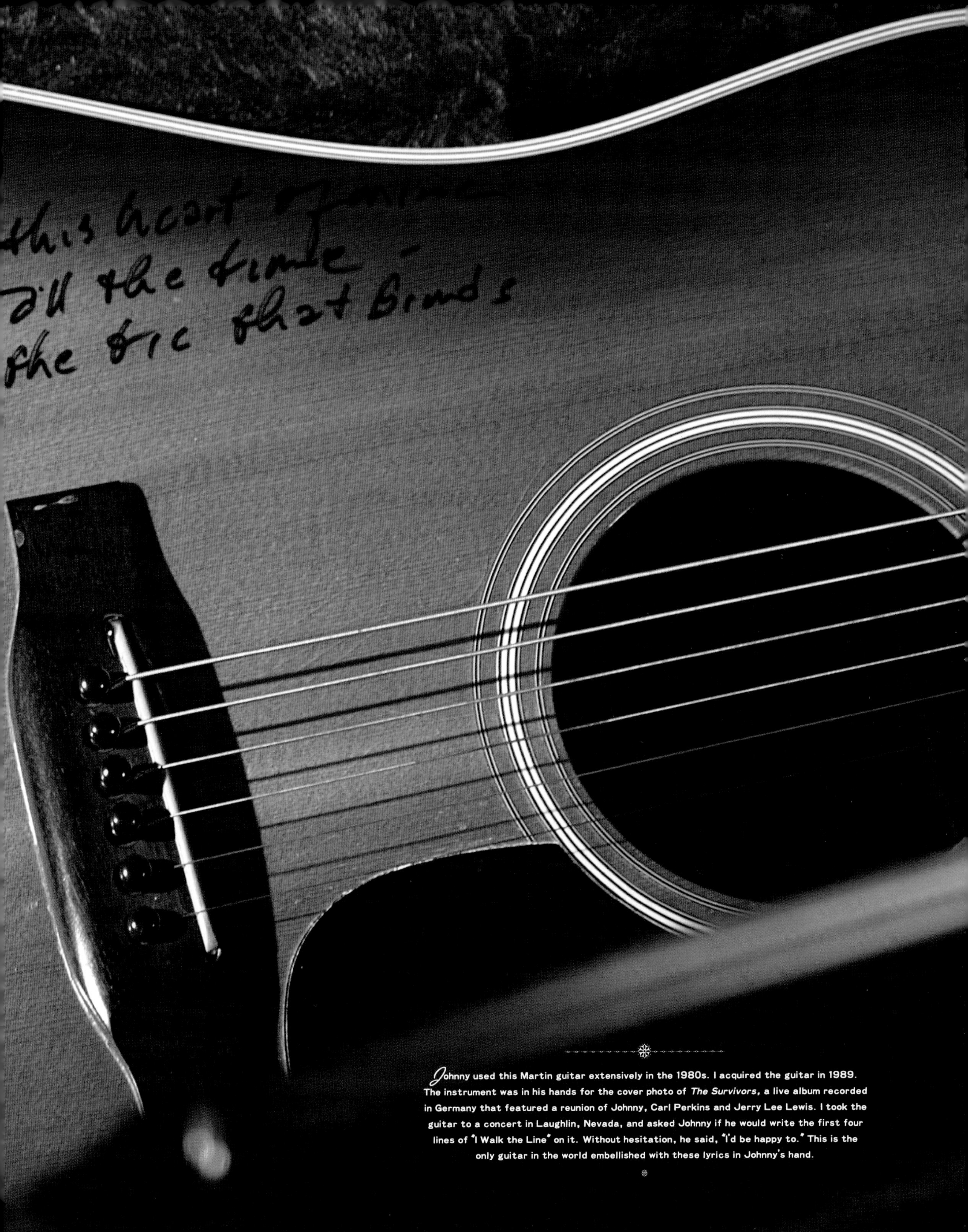

this heart of mine
all the time –
the tie that binds

Johnny used this Martin guitar extensively in the 1980s. I acquired the guitar in 1989.
The instrument was in his hands for the cover photo of *The Survivors*, a live album recorded
in Germany that featured a reunion of Johnny, Carl Perkins and Jerry Lee Lewis. I took the
guitar to a concert in Laughlin, Nevada, and asked Johnny if he would write the first four
lines of "I Walk the Line" on it. Without hesitation, he said, "I'd be happy to." This is the
only guitar in the world embellished with these lyrics in Johnny's hand.

During the 1960s and 1970s, record companies occasionally produced brightly colored promotional copies of an artist's latest release to get the attention of disc jockeys.

In 1973, I was 13 years old and my family was living in New Mexico when I found out the Johnny Cash Show was coming to Colorado. I had been a fan for five years, but I had never seen him in concert. By the time I got up the nerve to ask my dad if he'd drive me five hours to the Denver Auditorium, only the worst seats were available. My dad knew my passion for Johnny, so he agreed to let me try to get closer to the stage. As I reached the main floor, Johnny was singing "Orange Blossom Special," a song in which he used two harmonicas for the instrumental bridge. I was near the stage as he finished the song, and I raised my Kodak Hawkeye Instamatic camera. I saw this huge, awesome man above me, and as we made eye contact, he tossed me one of the harmonicas. I froze as it came my way. I was so overwhelmed that I walked out into the lobby to calm down. Standing there, awaiting her cue to go onstage, was June Carter. I had a large fan club button on my shirt, and as I made my way over to her, she said, "Well hi there, son. What's your name?" June was as gracious in that moment as she would be every time I saw her over the next 30 years. I don't recall my full response, but I replied, "Billy Miller" as she signed my badge.

The
Legend

JOHNNY CASH
MEMBERSHIP

Fan Club

This Card Entitles the Bearer

PEGGY BARNHART

to all membership privileges of the

JOHNNY CASH FAN CLUB

PRESIDENT—*Betty Siegfried*

HONORARY PRESIDENT—*Johnny Cash*

433 E. Main St.
Ventura, California   4/11/63 DUES $1.00

ALL OVER AGAIN
WHAT DO I CARE

DON'T TAKE YOUR GUNS TO TOWN BILL

ONE MORE RIDE
THAT'S ENOUGH

```
+-----------------------------------------------+
|  +-----------------------------------------+  |
|  |                                         |  |
|  |            JOURNAL #2                    |  |
|  |                                         |  |
|  |         FEATURING  OUR  STAR            |  |
|  |                                         |  |
|  |         J O H N N Y   C A S H           |  |
|  |                                         |  |
|  +-----------------------------------------+  |
+-----------------------------------------------+
```

❋

Johnny's popularity led to the formation of a fan club, started in 1959 by a family friend, Pat Isom. She produced several journals before turning over the club to someone better capable of handling the rapidly growing membership roll. The first two journals were created when the club had only a handful of members. They were produced on a mimeograph machine and hand-assembled with small photos pasted on the pages.

Each journal included a personal message from Johnny and his first wife, Vivian, and information on new record releases, upcoming performances and copies of press stories and reviews. The fans were exhorted to call radio stations and request that Johnny's songs be played, to buy his records for gifts, and to tell all their friends and neighbors about the new, hot and talented young singer.

❋

EUROPEAN
JOHNNY CASH
FANCLUB

EUROPEAN
JOHNNY CASH FAN CLUB
Postbus 17, 7720 AA Dalfsen
Holland

Jan Flederus

THE TROUBADOR

PICKIN' TIME

I STILL MISS SOMEONE

$\mathcal{I}$n the late 1960s, Johnny's sister, Reba, ran his fan club as the Johnny Cash Society. Charles and Virginia Stohler, a retired couple from Indiana, took over the club in the early 1970s and renamed it the Johnny and June Carter Cash International Fan Club. I joined the club in 1972 and became the Youth Editor of the club newsletter. I wrote a column called "Youth News and Views" from a preteen and teen perspective. After the club was disbanded in the late 1990s, Johnny requested that my website, JohnnyCash.com, serve as his official online presence and de facto fan club. In the days after Johnny's death, an average of 300 users per second visited JohnnyCash.com. At the time, it was the most traffic ever recorded on a celebrity website.

❅

JOURNAL #1
FEATURING OUR STAR
JOHNNY CASH

JOHNNY CASH
Box 5056
Memphis, Tenn.

Dear Club Members:

    Here is our first journal. It's just a start, but we hope it will be informative and entertaining. Our club president, Pat Isom, has spent many long hours working on it, and a lot of you have contributed to it, which we appreciate very much.

    About our tours: Recently we have been to the Maritime Provinces of Canada, Nova Scotia, New Brunswick, and Prince Edward Island. On this tour we had along some of our buddies from Wheeling, West Virginia, Red Allen and the Osborne Bros., Johnny Six and Don Helms. I think we had more fun than the audiences. These fellows have become some of our very best friends, and the people love them.

    Following that tour, we went west to Texas, New Mexico, Arizona with Don Gibson, one of our favorite singers, Danny and the Juniors, Roy Orbison, and Sonny Burgess. Everyone knows Danny and the Juniors for their record, "At the Hop". They added quite a bit of variety to the show. Roy Orbison is, of course, an old friend who visits with us often. To steal a Homer and Jethro joke - he comes to our house every Sunday and next Sunday I think we're gonna let him eat. Roy is one of the finest songwriters in the business, having written "Claudette", "Down the Line" and many other hits. By the way, Roy's wife's name is Claudette. Sonny Burgess, Memphis' new rock and roll singer will also be with us on a two week's tour of the West Coast starting June 19th.

    Have you heard Freddie Hart's latest record called "I Won't Be Home Tonight"? It's a fine record and Freddie Hart is one of the most sincere, most talented people in this business.

    We have a new release out shortly. An extended play 45 rpm album called "JOHNNY CASH SINGS HANK WILLIAMS". We did it as a sort of tribute to Hank. We hope you enjoy the four songs.

    Watch us on our third appearance on Dick Clarks' show July 5th. The day before have yourself a happy 4th of July, and again, many many thanks for the help.

                         Gratefully,

                         Johnny Cash

THE JOHNNY CASH SHOW

PERSONNEL
ADMIT BACKSTAGE

ARTIST CONSULTANTS PRODUCTIONS

It's hard to describe my thrill when I received my first
all-access backstage pass in 1974. I was 14. This pass, issued
by Johnny's manager, Lou Robin, allowed me to visit Johnny
whenever I could talk my parents or their friends into
driving me to a show. This pass got a lot of use and
helped me get to know Johnny.

ON STAGE!

"*America's Most Versatile Entertainer*"

JOHNNY CASH

Bringing you the finest in Folk and Country Talent!

AND FEATURING . . .

...RKINS • MARSHALL GRANT

This photograph features the true pioneers of rock 'n' roll: (left to right) Jerry Lee Lewis, Carl Perkins, Elvis Presley and Johnny Cash. Taken in the legendary Sun Recording Studio in Memphis, Tennessee, the shot immortalized what would come to be known as the Million Dollar Quartet. This gathering of the boys was not planned. Perkins was recording an album, with Lewis playing piano in the session. Presley dropped by with a girlfriend, and Cash stopped in while on a shopping errand. When Sun Records founder Sam Phillips realized that four of his top stars were in the studio, he flipped the tape recorder on and let it run while the boys did an impromptu sing-along. Although a record of the session was never officially released, some songs from the session have shown up in the market. Johnny left early in the session, which explains his absence on most of the songs that have surfaced. This print was signed for me by the surviving members in 1994. I had a black pen, but Lewis signed in red. When it was Perkins's turn, he said, "Don't worry about the different colors. Johnny signed in black, Lewis is famous for 'Great Balls of Fire,' which makes the red work, so I'll sign in blue for my song, 'Blue Suede Shoes.' It's perfect."
The photographer who captured the image has never claimed credit. I asked Johnny if he knew who took the shot. He narrowed it down to a couple of Memphis press photographers. He also told me that if the photo hadn't been cropped there would have been a fifth person visible.
According to Johnny, Presley's girlfriend was at the end of the piano.

APRIL 1963

18 - Fort Dodge, Iowa - Laramar Ballroom
19 - Moline, Illinois - Wharton Fieldhouse
20 - Decatur, Illinois - Kintner Gymnasium
21 - Freeport, Illinois - Consistory Auditorium
23 - Rockford, Illinois - Coronado Theatre
24 - Grand Forks, North Dakota - Univ. of N. D.
25 - Fargo, North Dakota - Municipal Auditorium
26 - Duluth, Minnesota - Armory
27 - Milwaukee, Wisconsin - Civic Auditorium
28 - Chicago, Illinois - Arie Crown Theatre

MAY 1963

14 - Miami, Florida - Dade Auditorium
15 - Orlando, Florida - Auditorium
16 - Macon, Georgia - City Auditorium
17 - Columbus, Georgia
18 - Columbia, South Carolina
19 - Greensboro, North Carolina
23 - New London, Connecticut
24 - Providence, Rhode Island
25 - Boston, Massachusetts
26 - Bangor, Maine

JUNE 1963

14 - Atlanta, Georgia
15 - Shreveport, Louisiana - Municipal Auditorium
16 - Houston, Texas - Sam Houston Coliseum
17 - Dallas, Texas
18 - Austin, Texas
19 - San Antonio, Texas
20 - El Paso, Texas (2)
21 - Fresno, California (2)
22 - Hollywood, California
23 - Sacramento, California

JULY 1963

- Urbana

Jill sweep out your —
yes and I will bring you water
yes and I will bring you music
So you'll never be alone

I will bring you honey
from the bee tree in the meadow
I'll go dig in diamond mines
And bring you the biggest stone

HOPE

"Everybody should be able to get a
little help when they need it."

JRC

On a summer night in the 1960s, the Johnny Cash Show
was in town for a performance at the local high school
gymnasium, just another stop on the long dusty trail for
the touring musicians. As townspeople filled the place
and the air became electric with anticipation, the troupe
realized that the star was missing.

Tommy Cash, who was part of the show, walked the
halls and checked the classrooms in search of his brother.
The last place he looked was the boys' locker room.
He found Johnny walking slowly and peering deliberately
into each of the mesh-wire lockers, a rolled $100 bill
tucked between his thumb and index finger.

"What are you doing? The show's about to start," Tommy said.

"I'm looking for the dirtiest, rattiest tennis shoes I can find,"
Johnny said. "I figure the boy could use this."

Folsom Prison Blues

① I hear the train 's comin'
It's rollin' round the bend
And I aint seen the sunshine
Since I don't know when
I'm stuck in Folsom Prison and time keeps draggin on
But that train keeps rollin on down to San Antone

② When I was just a baby
My mama told me son
Always be a good boy
Don't ever play with guns
But I shot a man in Reno just to watch him die
When I hear that whistle blowing I hang my head and cry

③ I bet there's rich folks eatin'
In a fancy dinin' car
They're probably drinkin coffee
And smokin' big cigars
I know I had it comin' I know I cant be free
But those people keep a movin' and thats what tortures me

④ If they freed me from this prison
If that railroad train was mine
I bet I'd move it on
A little farther down the line
Far from Folsom Prison thats where I want to stay
And I'd let that lonesome whistle blow my blues away

Johny Cash
1955

46

In the early 1990s, Johnny agreed that I would take over his souvenir business and produce items for sale to his fans. He wasn't interested in doing mass-produced things like key chains, baseball caps and the typical stuff that had been offered for years, so he asked me to develop a few items. I decided to concentrate on high-end collectibles. I found some great early photographs for autographing, had reproductions made of a painting he'd done, gathered harmonicas he'd played onstage, and bought every original copy of his first Sun record I could find. I also dreamed of having Johnny handwrite, in a very limited edition, the lyrics to a few of his best-known compositions. He was crazy about the items. "This is really classy," he said. Preparing the collectibles went smoothly, except for the lyrics. Being a man of high energy, Johnny rarely sat in one place or did one thing very long. He did two or three copies of each song and got bored with the process. His manager, Lou Robin, called me and said he would send some of the lyrics that Johnny had completed. When I opened the box, I had to smile. My unpredictable friend had completed a few sets of lyrics, but he also had embellished them in his own inimitable fashion. On several of the "Folsom Prison Blues" lyrics, he had traced his huge hand. On a copy of "I Walk the Line," he had traced an outline of his bare foot. That was the first—and last—delivery of handwritten lyrics I received. I understood Johnny's schedule made it impossible for him to write out each song. But this is one of those efforts.

"EVERYBODY
WAS WEARING RHINESTONES,
ALL THOSE SPARKLE CLOTHES
AND COWBOY BOOTS.
I DECIDED TO WEAR A
BLACK SHIRT AND PANTS
AND SEE IF I COULD GET BY
WITH IT. I DID AND I'VE
WORN BLACK CLOTHES
EVER SINCE."

JOHNNY CASH

In preparation for Johnny's concert at San Quentin Prison on February 24, 1969, inmates who worked in the printshop made posters announcing the event. This is one of the only copies known to exist. Notice the "Best Behavior Advised" admonition. Johnny wore the custom-made blue jumpsuit shown on pages 52—53 when he rehearsed for the concert. He had it on when photographer Jim Marshall snapped the unforgettable image of Johnny flipping the bird to the Granada Television crew that filmed the concert for British TV. Johnny also wore the jumpsuit for rehearsals for his ABC-TV series, including one with Bob Dylan. Prior to traveling to San Quentin, Johnny received a song from Shel Silverstein that Silverstein hoped Johnny would sing during the concert. Onstage, Johnny mentioned the song and remarked, "I'm anxious to hear it. I don't know how it's gonna sound." Reading the lyrics from the sheet on his music stand, Johnny made it through "A Boy Named Sue" on the first take. The song was included on the live album from the concert and became one of Johnny's biggest hits. The *Johnny Cash at San Quentin* album helped make Johnny a household name throughout the world. Some think it's the greatest live record ever made.

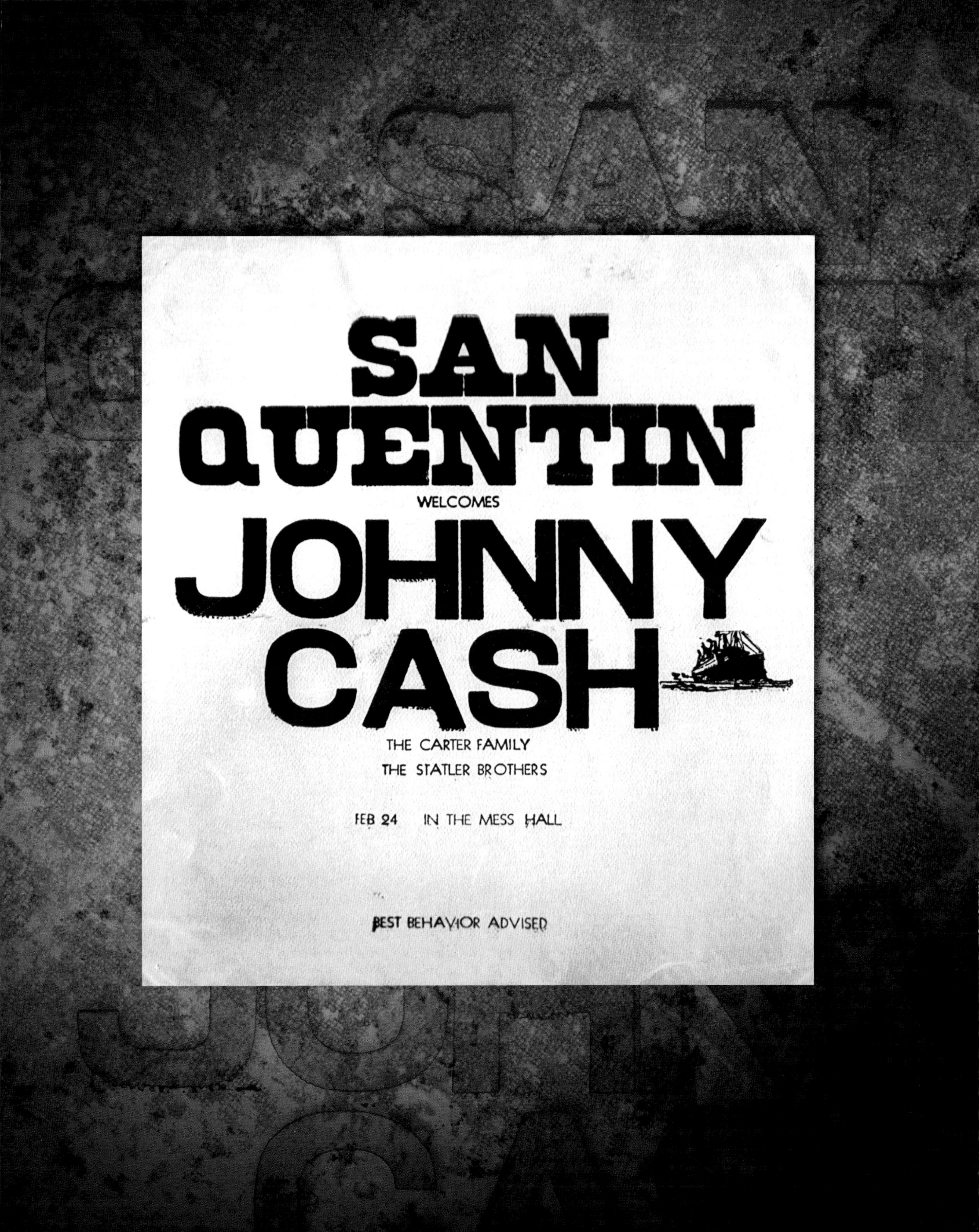

SAN QUENTIN

WELCOMES

JOHNNY CASH

THE CARTER FAMILY

THE STATLER BROTHERS

FEB 24   IN THE MESS HALL

BEST BEHAVIOR ADVISED

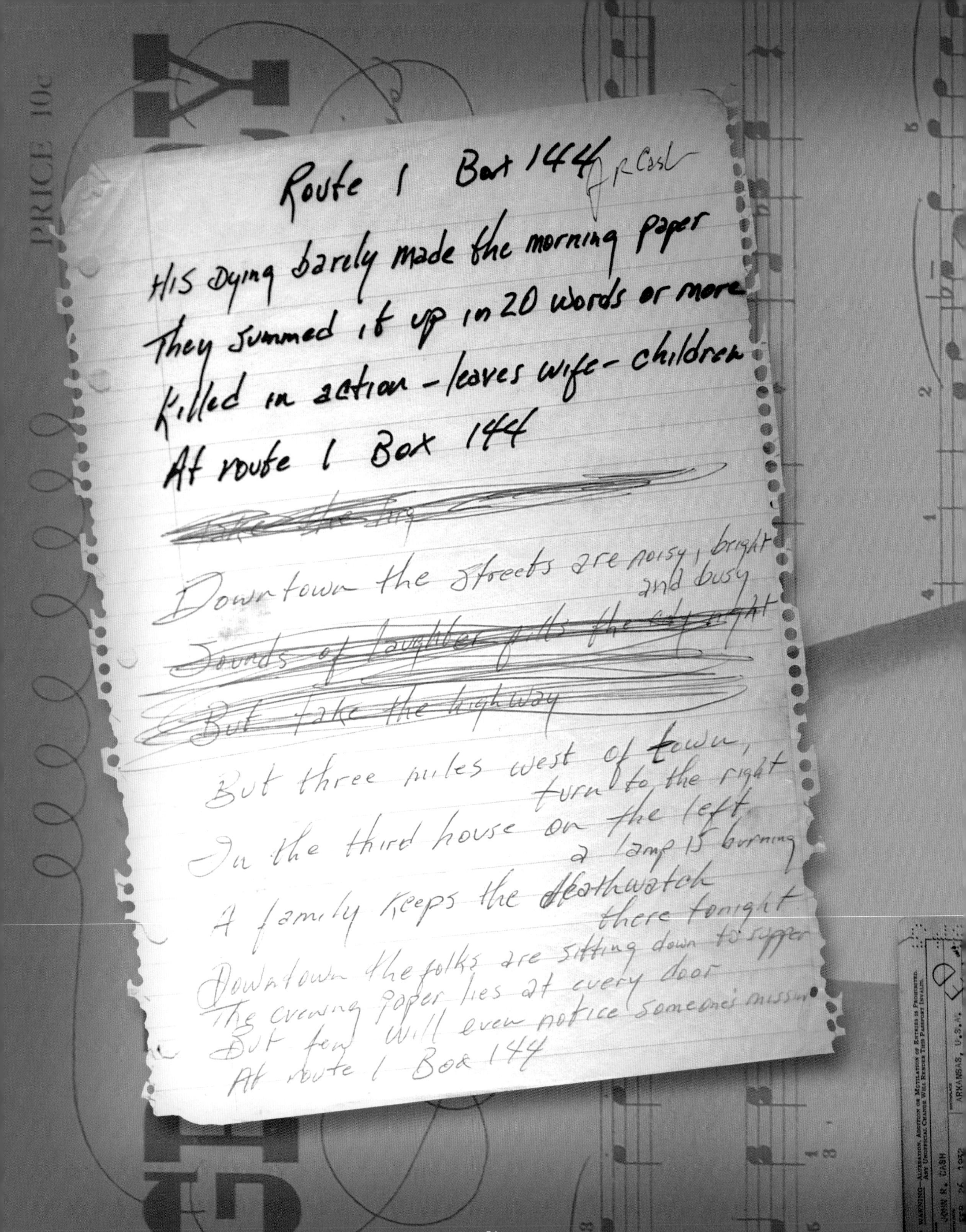

Route 1   Box 144   J R Cash

His dying barely made the morning paper
They summed it up in 20 words or more
Killed in action — leaves wife — children
At route 1 Box 144

~~Take the ring~~

~~Downtown the streets are noisy, bright~~
~~and busy~~
~~Sounds of laughter fills the street~~ ~~night~~
~~But take the highway~~

But three miles west of town,
          turn to the right
In the third house on the left
          a lamp is burning
A family keeps the deathwatch
          there tonight

Downtown the folks are sitting down to supper
The evening paper lies at every door
But few will even notice someone's missin
At route 1 Box 144

The newsreports tell many kinds of stories
Each day, of things some famous man has done
Deeds of goodness, kindness, even greatness;
Important people, known by everyone.
But everyone means something to somebody
And out there where the wreath is on the door
~~The missing is the worlds biggest person~~
~~At route line, Box 144~~

The Worlds most important persons
At rt 1 Box 144 missing

JOHNNY CASH
200 Caudill
Hendersonville
Tn. 37075

THE
JOHNNY
CASH
SHOW

GALLATIN RD.
HENDERSONVILLE, TENN.

J.C.

Johnny traveled with this monogrammed briefcase in
the late 1970s. He wrote his name and home address on
one of the identification tags. I often saw Johnny carrying
this briefcase, and it stirs many memories. He would
open the case and show me photographs he'd taken
and songs he'd written.

Oct 15 1964

Dear Rosane Kathleen, Cindy
& Tara,

Hi Babies! I love you.
I am sorry that I
have to be away so long.
I miss you so much, and
I hope you still love me
even though I don't
get to talk to you
often.

"Hurricane Isabell" is not far from here, but it is going some other way. The weather is fine here. I am OK. I will talk to you when I can.

Be sweet and dont forget that I love you. Study hard, and be good girls.

All my love
Daddy.

SUNDAY	MONDAY	TUESDAY	WEDNESDAY
			1
5 *Chicago* ~~scribble~~	6 ~~HBO~~ *Wash DC*	7 ~~scribble~~ ~~HBO~~ *Wash DC*	8 ~~scribble~~ 15 Ⓦ
12	13	14 ~~scribble~~	
19 EASTER PASSOVER Ⓦ ROTTERDAM HOLLAND Ⓦ	20 LONDON ENG. Ⓦ	21 Ⓦ ~~scribble~~ OFF	22 PARIS, FR.
26 Ⓦ *Zurich Switz*	27 Ⓦ	28	29 *Montreux*

THINGS TO DO TODAY!   Date:_____

Urgent   Done ✓

1. Not Smoke
2. Kiss June
3. Not Kiss anyone else
4. Cough
5. Pee
6. Eat
7. Not eat too much
8. Worry
9. Go See Mama.
10. Practice Piano

NOTES:

Not write notes

FREE
JOHNNY CASH RECORD
"IT AIN'T ME BABE"
COMPLIMENTARY RECORD WHEN YOU BUY THIS CAN OF Snowdrift
JOHNNY CASH HEARD EXCLUSIVELY ON COLUMBIA RECORDS

Country & Western

RECORD

REVIEW

PUBLISHED MONTHLY

30¢

JOHNNY

Album Releases by Johnny Cash

SLP 1220 "Hot and Blue Guitar"
Side One — Rock Island Line, Lonesome Whistle, Country Boy, If You Good Lord's will-. So Doggone Lonesome, I walk the line. Cry Cry Cry. Remember the line.
Side Two — When I happened to walk the '97, Folsom Prison Blues, Doin' my time.

SLP 1235 "Songs that made him famous"
Side One — Ballad of a teenage queen, There you go, I walk the line, Don't make me go. Guess things happen that way, Next in line. Train of love, a woman in love, Next to Heaven.
Side Two — Ways of love, Your the nearest thing to Heaven, I can't help it. Home of the Blues. Big river.

SLP 1240 "Greatest Johnny Cash"
Side One — Goodbye little Darlin', I just thought you'd like to know. You tell me. Just about time, I forgot to remember to forget, Katy, Too.
Side Two — Thanks a lot, Luther's boogie, You win again, Hey good lookin', I could never be ashamed of you, Get Rhythm.

SLP 1245 "Johnny Cash sings Hank Williams"
Side One — I can't help it, You win again, Hey good lookin', I could never be ashamed of you. Next in line, Straight A's in Love.
Side Two — Folsom Prison Blues, Give my Love to Rose, I walk the line, I love you because, Come in Stranger, Mean Eyed Cat.

SLP 1255 "Now Here's Johnny Cash"
Side One — Sugartime, Down the street to 301, Life goes on, Port of Lonely Hearts, Cry Cry Cry, My Treasure.
Side Two — Oh Lonesome me So doggone lone-some, You're the nearest thing to Heaven, Story of a broken heart, Hey Porter, Home of the blues.

U.K. PHILIPS and CBS releases

Philips, BBL 7381 "Songs of our soil"
Side One —

Philips, BBL 7373 "Hymns by Johnny Cash"
Side One — It was Jesus, I saw a man, Are all the children in, The old account was settled, Lead me gently home, Swing low sweet chariot.
Side Two — Snow in his hair, Lead me Father, I call him, These things shall pass, He'll be a friend, God will.

Philips, BBL 7417 "Ride this train"
Side One — Loading coal, Slow rider, Lumberjack, Dorraine of Ponchartrain.
Side Two — Goin' to Memphis, When papa played the Dobro, Boss Jack, Old Doc Brown.

Philips, BBL 7298 "The Fabulous Johnny Cash"
Side One — Run softly Blue River, Frankie's man Johnny, That's all over, That I found out, One more ride.
Side Two — I still miss someone, Don't take your guns to town, I'd rather die young, Pickin' time, Shepherd of my heart, Supper time.

Philips, BBL 7358 "Now there was a song"
Side One — Seasons of my heart, I feel better all over, I couldn't keep from crying. Time changes everything, My lovin' keep walking back to you, I'd just be a fool enough to fall.
Side Two — Transfusion blues, Why do you punish me, I will miss you when you're gone, I'm so lonesome I could cry, Just one more, Honky tonk girl.

CBS, BPG 62015 "Hymns from the Heart"
Side One — He'll understand and say well done, God must have my fortune laid down, When I've learned, I got down on the lower lights be burning, Let us meet again.
Side Two — When I take my vacation in Heaven, When he reached down to me, Taller than the trees, he said to me, to cross Jordan alone, My God I wish. These hands.

CBS, BPG 62073 "The Sound of Johnny Cash"
Side One — Lost on the Desert, Accidentally on purpose, In the Jailhouse now, Lonesome, You aren't love to in them old cottonfields back home.
Side Two — Delia's gone I forgot more than ever know, Yet someone tell me, free from the chain gang now, down easy. Sing a going

---

Johnny Cash

COUNTRY ARTISTS ARE UNIQUE

A phenomenon unique to the Country Music field is the composer who is the most successful singer of his own songs. The most gifted — and successful — example in recent years is Columbia's 26 year-old Johnny Cash, whose hit recordings of his own compositions have appeared repeatedly on national best-seller charts. He is endowed with a vibrant, supple baritone voice and the best folk-poetic writing talent since the late Hank Williams, laureate of the country field.

Biggest of all the Johnny Cash records has been "I Walk The Line" which catapulted him into the national spotlight just a few years ago. More than fifty Cash songs have been recorded by such widely varying stars as Jimmy Wakely, Rusty Draper, Hoagy Car-michael, Ernest Tubb, and Lawrence Welk. What more appeal could a songwriter have? Since his first record of "Cry, Cry, Cry" and "Hey, Porter", he has appeared with Marty Robbins, Ray Price, Carl Perkins and others on "Grand Ole Opry" as well as on such net-work shows as Ed Sullivan's "Toast of the Town". His debut Columbia single record, "What Do I Care" and "All Over Again", a hit, of course, was followed by an album, "The Fabulous Johnny Cash".

As a child in Kingsland, Arkansas Johnny sang hymns almost constantly — with his family, while doing his chores on the farm. In high school he achieved local renown for his renditions of Joyce Kilmer's **Trees** and **Because.**

Soon after High School graduation Johnny joined the Air Force and was sent to Germany.

During his three-year stay there, Johnny played and sang countless impromptu musi-cales on the base and in small German clubs. His objective was not, however, a musical career. Once out of the Air Force, Johnny enrolled in a radio and television school with high hopes of becoming an announcer, but a lack of finances necessitated a change in plans.

Johnny sold electrical appliances instead and saved his vocalizing for after working

hours. By this time he found himself in Memphis, Tennessee where a local boy named Elvis Presley was gaining success with a local company, Sun Records. Johnny went to see the label's president, Sam Phillips, who sug-gested ballads might be suitable material for records. So Johnny simply wrote a couple, recorded them, watched his first hit record mushroom and has been repeating the success cycle ever since.

Recently versatile Johnny has taken off in a new direction. He is studying dramatics, with an eye to television and movies.

11

MANILA ☼ HILTON

How do you like the people
How do you like this place
If it were me
It hurt to see
An old familiar face

WARNING—ALTERATION, ADDITION OR MUTILATION OF ENTRIES IS PROHIBITED. ANY UNOFFICIAL CHANGE WILL RENDER THIS PASSPORT INVALID.
JUNE CARTER NIX
VIRGINIA, U.S.A.
BLUE
JUNE 23, 1929
BROWN
ISSUE DATE
OCT. 16, 1961
PASSPORT RENEWAL
5
5½
X X X
X X X
June Carter Nix
IMPORTANT: THIS PASSPORT EXPIRES THREE YEARS FROM ISSUE DATE UNLESS OTHERWISE LIMITED. IF RENEWED, IT EXPIRES FIVE YEARS FROM ISSUE DATE.
Photograph of bearer
June Carter Nix

JOHNNY AND JUNE'S RELATIONSHIP SERVED AS A MODEL OF WHAT A GOOD MARRIAGE SHOULD BE.

Over the years, I saw them in many different situations, and I was always taken by their devotion to each other. They were funny together, in a sweet and endearing fashion. Johnny would start to tell a story, and sometimes June would interrupt with one of hers. He'd never get upset or even shoot a cross look at her; he'd just wait for her to finish and then continue with his story. They had a charming and friendly competition about them. As highly successful entertainers, each had a dose of ego, although not in a remotely offensive way. I'd ask Johnny how many copies of his book had sold, and June would proceed to tell me about her book's success. They loved to hang out together, cuddle up together, shop together and perform together. You could see Johnny light up when June joined him onstage. As many times as they performed their onstage routines, the love they displayed kept their act from ever growing stale. Near the end of June's life, Johnny was very sick, and she would sit with him, hold his hand, and read to him from the Bible and other books. When June died, I knew that Johnny would never get over the loss. They were one in the truest sense of the word. They depended on each other, enduring struggles and handling triumphs that most of us could never begin to fathom. Their union was a rarity in the entertainment world.

IT STOOD THE TEST OF TIME, SURVIVED THE WORST OF TIMES, AND PROVED THAT TRUE LOVE CONQUERS ALL.

To June, This morning

The night was cold as Dawson
~~then in the~~

Then Dawned a short white day
The brave sun rose lightning hot
And singing climbed its way
The lake with mist was shrouded
~~...~~ Grandfather east wind blew
The mist froze on the treelimbs
And I arose ahead of you

I made the morning coffee
Then your feet on the stair
You said Good morning to me
Then I sat beside you there

My head in happy blouzed
For love lives in this house

7 AM Feb 4 1970

Johnny CASH

America's "Most Played"*
Folk Singer & Writer

*Cash Box Po
(Cash   58)

record-   -59 - U. S. - Canada - Australia

Johnny and June released "If I Were a Carpenter" in December 1969.
The song peaked at number 2 on the charts and became a staple in
every concert they did together. When they sang it in the early 1990s,
June would break into a dance that featured Egyptian-like moves, much
to the delight of audiences. June stopped doing the dance in 1992, but
when I asked her at a show in Las Vegas in August of that year if she would do
it again that night, she readily agreed. June again brought down the house
with her dance. After the show, when I was alone with Johnny, I asked why
June had stopped doing the dance, considering that it was so popular.
"She's been having excruciating back pain," he said, as I turned beet red.
June was a grand lady and the consummate professional.

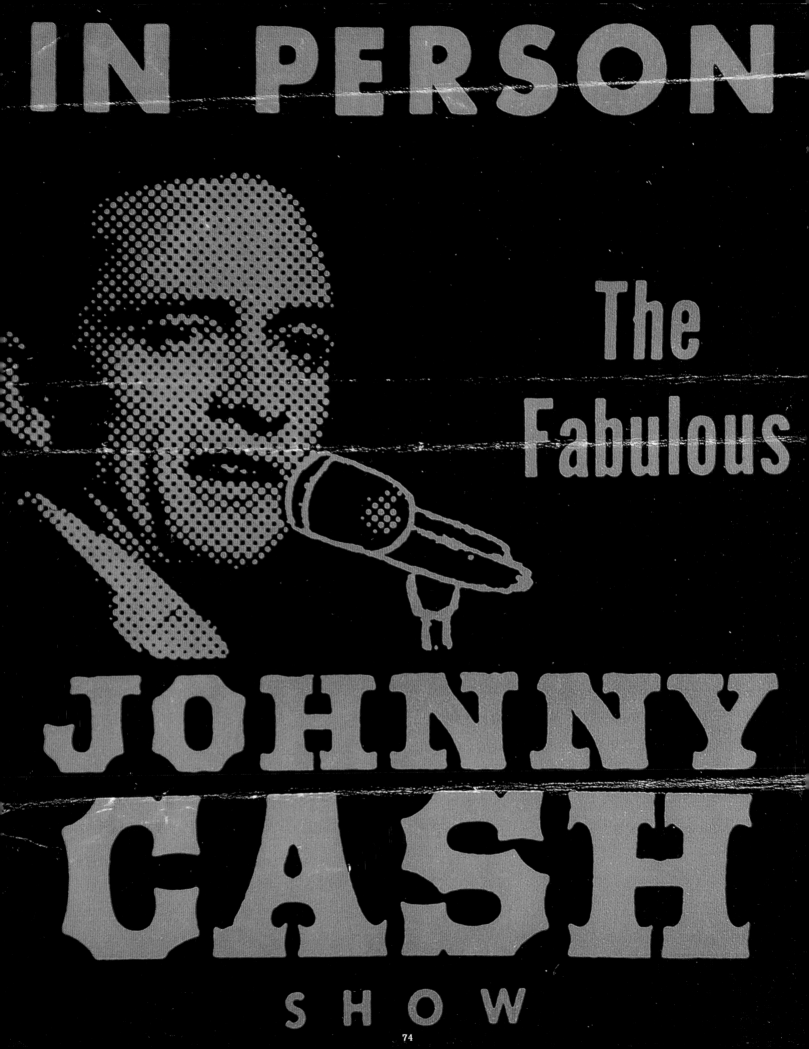

IN PERSON

The
Fabulous

JOHNNY
CASH
SHOW

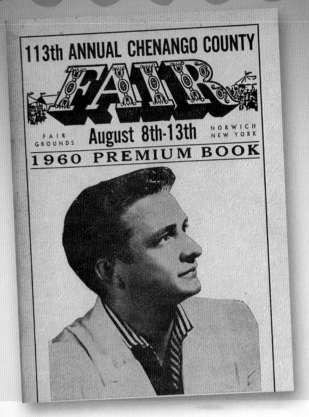

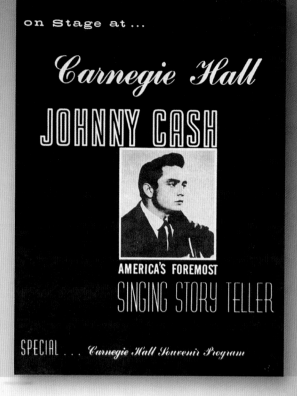

For the thousands of shows that Johnny performed around the world over nearly five decades, there were thousands of programs made for the fans. Some were produced by the Johnny Cash organization; others by the venue or promoter. The most elaborate ones were the official programs created under the direct supervision of Johnny. Programs from the mid-1970s included photography of people, places and things taken by Johnny with his Nikon camera. Each photo was accompanied by a reproduction of Johnny's handwritten caption, along with anecdotes when he felt further comment was necessary. I think Johnny enjoyed it whenever a new official program was produced, since he was able to showcase new photographs he'd taken.

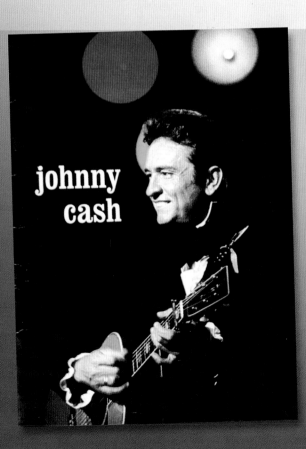

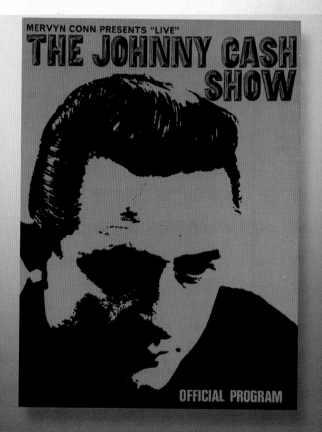

The final INTERVIEW

I had met Chuck Berry, Fats Domino, Little Richard, Jerry Lee Lewis, all the pioneer rock & roll guys. But I'd never met Johnny Cash until August 20th, 2003, when I made my way out to his house on Old Hickory Lake, about a half hour outside of Nashville, to interview him.

The house, in which Cash had lived for the past thirty years, was a big, sprawling place filled with many rooms and much memorabilia: framed hit records, personal letters from several U.S. presidents, seventy-some guitars, 16 signed Norman Rockwell lithographs, and what seemed like endless collections of plates, platters, glasses, goblets, and ornate silver services. (Tableware was a longtime passion of Johnny's wife, June, who'd died the previous May at the age of 73).

All of these things would eventually be passing into the hands of various friends and family members. Very soon, actually, as it turned out.

Johnny was extremely ill. At the age of 71, he was white-haired and withered by years of diabetes, asthma, and glaucoma. To make his way from an upstairs bedroom down to the ground floor, where our interview was to take place, required both a wheelchair and a specially installed elevator, which, with its all-around Plexiglass windows, Johnny referred to as his "popemobile." He descended in this contraption like some half-departed monarch turning back for one last earthly curtain call. He was dressed, as always, in black. A clutch of people fondly fluttered and fussed around him, and finally he maneuvered himself into a chair in camera position. It was understood that our interview would be brief: Johnny tired easily and had difficulty speaking; he stopped frequently to sip from a glass of homemade iced tea. In the end, he was able to give us 30 minutes of his diminishing time.

I'm a great fan of Johnny Cash's music, especially the early Sun Records singles, like "I Walk the Line" and "Home of the Blues" and "I Guess Things Happen That Way." But I'd never really thought of him as being in the first rank of the early rock & rollers. His music was a little too spare, his rumbling baritone a little too deadpan, his stage manner a little too reserved (or maybe it was a little too country). He lacked Chuck Berry's epochal guitar and Fats Domino's radiant warmth; and compared to Little Richard and Jerry Lee Lewis, he seemed almost reticent. (Although God knows he had some famously wild times offstage).

But what's the point of ranking artists in this way? Johnny Cash differed from people like Richard and Jerry Lee in the same way he differed from every other rock or pop or country star: He was unique, a category unto himself. Nobody else ever sounded like Johnny Cash, or produced such an extensive and memorable and often haunting body of work so unassumingly, and with such minimal means.

The occasion of our interview was Johnny's nomination for several MTV Video Music Awards for "Hurt," a stunning, autumnal video directed by Mark Romanek. Music videos can be many things, most of them technological. But very rarely do they move us emotionally. "Hurt," a heart-shredding portrait of Johnny Cash at the end of his life, did this. It was like no other video anyone had ever seen.

Johnny was looking forward to flying to New York for the Video Music Awards, but at the last minute he had to go back in the hospital, and so couldn't come. He'd also been planning to fly out to Los Angeles to start work with producer Rick Rubin on another of the stark and singular albums that had brought him to the attention of a new generation in recent years. He didn't make that flight, either.

I'm glad I finally got to meet him, or at least to stand in his presence, even just once. The man was a monument, and I wish I'd met him in his prime. Three weeks after this interview, he was dead.

— Kurt Loder , 2004

Loder: How big is your studio?

Cash: Well, it's big enough. It was a log cabin and we converted it into a studio and then we added a room for musicians. It's adequate. I've never really believed in a ballroom-sized studio.

Loder: What kind of studio do you record in with Rick Rubin?

Cash: We record at his house. In an even smaller studio.

Loder: You have been nominated for six MTV Video Music Awards. How does that make you feel?

Cash: Kinda overwhelmed. I'm very grateful for the nominations and all of the votes.

Loder: Do you enjoy the video process?

Cash: Not especially.

Loder: Why not?

Cash: It's just work. Sometimes it's really fun, and I enjoy it very much, usually. But the getting there and all that. . . I enjoyed doing the "Hurt" video because I felt like we were doing something worthwhile. It was something really special.

Loder: Who came up with the concept for that video?

Cash: Mark Romanek, the director.

Loder: It's a heart-wrenching, personal video. How did you feel about it?

Cash: Well, as you say, personal. I was there personally, right in the middle of the thing. After it was put together, I watched it with kind of a critical eye to see what I could find wrong with it. I didn't find much wrong with it at all, and I called Mark and told him that it was a job well done. I was proud of it. And the same with Rick Rubin. I called Rick and I told him that I appreciated his input, that I felt like it was a very good video. So I was happy about it from the very beginning.

Loder: Were you emotional when you performed the song?

Cash: Yeah, I felt very emotional doing it.

Loder: What were your thoughts the first time you heard "Hurt?"

Cash: Rick played the song for me. When I heard the record, I said, "I can't do that song. It's not my style." He said, "Well, let's just try it another way. Let me do something." So he put down a track, and I listened to it. From there, we started working on it until we got the record made.

Loder: The video told so much. It seemed to be you looking back on your career and accomplishments. You seemed to be saying, "This doesn't mean much in the light of eternity, in the light of mortality."

Cash: Exactly. It's all fleeting, as fame is fleeting. So are all the trappings of fame, all the money, the clothes, the furniture, of which I have lots.

Loder: Looking back on what you have done, do you have any regrets?

Cash: I used to, but I forgave myself. When God forgave me, I figured I better do it, too. So everything is all right now.

Loder: Are you familiar with Eminem, the rap musician?

Cash: Yeah . . .

Loder: He often comes under criticism because he does songs about death and murder and drugs. I know you've done a lot of songs of death and murder, and some drugs, too. Were you criticized for making those records?

Cash: I didn't get any direct criticism for "Hurt." I mean, I didn't have preachers calling me, nothing like that. But people that I'd expected to not especially like it, they let me know that they kind of turned a deaf ear to it, that I would be all right as long as I didn't play that video for them, that record for them. But most people, and I mean most people, 98 percent of them, were complimentary. My children, my grandchildren, they all love it, they're all proud of it.

Loder: "Folsom Prison Blues" is about someone getting shot. Did people criticize you for that sort of song back in the day?

Cash: Always have. I've always had that pointed up in my face, that I wrote a song with a line in it, "I shot a man in Reno just to watch him die." But, you know, I wasn't the first. In the late 1920s, country singer Jimmie Rodgers, in one of his Blue Yodeler songs, had a line that says, "I'm going to shoot poor Thelma just to see her jump and fall." He may have been the first to write a line like that, I don't know. But I wasn't thinking of Jimmie when I wrote it; I was thinking that I was in that prison. I just try to put myself in the place that I'm singing about.

Loder: Songs about death go way back. The Carter family did some, so it probably goes all the way back to Britain.

Cash: Oh yeah, there's a lot of bloody songs in the Carter family repertoire.

Loder: Young black men today are doing songs like that and coming under criticism for it. Do you have any advice for them?

Cash: Ignore it. Do what you do. You can't let people dictate to you what you should do when it's coming from way in here [pointing at his heart]. Somebody comes in your face with something, tells you what you ought to do, you can take them at their word or you can just turn your back. I wouldn't let anyone influence me into thinking I was doing the wrong thing by singing about death, hell and drugs because I've always done that and I always will.

Loder: You wanted to be a gospel singer, and you had a period when you were using drugs. Was that a spiritual crisis? Did you feel as if you had lost your way?

Cash: Yeah, I felt like I had lost my way. Let me have a drink of tea and I'll tell you the story.

Loder: I'll have a drink, too.

Cash: In 1967, I was on amphetamines really bad, and I was totally insane. I got in my Jeep and drove to Chattanooga. There's a cave there called Nickajack Cave. A monstrous cave, it goes on for miles back under Lookout Mountain. I went into that cave with my pills, just exploring. I had all these wild ideas about finding gold, Civil War relics or something in this cave. I kept going and going, and the cave kept getting bigger, and these big rooms with stalactites and stalagmites were there, and I would shine my light on them and imagine all kinds of things. I kept taking the amphetamines, and after I'd been in there about three hours—it seemed like three hours; it might have been less; it might have been more—I sat down and took more pills. And then I lay down and closed my eyes, or tried to close my eyes—you can't close your eyes for long on amphetamines—and said, "God, I can't take it anymore. I can't make it any further. You'll have to take me now. I want to go. I want to die." I closed my eyes and said, "I'm gonna die now." I've never said that God talked to me, but it seemed I heard his voice saying, "You're not going to die yet." I felt like God was telling me, "You're not going to die yet." So I sat up. I felt better. I felt sober. I got up and I did this old Indian trick [licking his finger and putting it in the air] to see which way the wind was blowing, and I followed that out to the entrance of the cave, and I got into my Jeep and went back home.

Loder: Was that the end of your dependence on amphetamines?

Cash: Well, it was the beginning of the end. A commissioner of mental health for the state of Tennessee was a friend of mine and June's, and June had him come out. He said, "If you are serious about getting off of amphetamines, I'll be here at your house every day at five o'clock." I said, "I'm serious," so he started coming. I stayed straight and sober, except for one day, and that one day he walked in the door and said, "How you doing?" And I said, "Great! Just great!" And he said, "The hell you are. You ain't great." And I said, "No sir, I'm not great." He caught me. Anyway, that was the beginning of the end. I did get off of amphetamines, and I stayed off for quite a long time.

Loder: June helped you with all that?

Cash: Oh, June was my solid rock. She was always there. She was my counselor, comforter, everything else. What a wonderful woman she was.

Loder: You were married for more than 30 years. What is the secret to maintaining a long relationship?

Cash: We were together for 40 years. We worked on the road together since 1963, and we got married in 1968. And the secret to a happy marriage: separate bathrooms.

Loder: That's it?

Cash: I think so.

Loder: Before June died, did she have any advice for you? Did she keep you going?

Cash: Oh yeah, she was my great encourager. She loved the "Hurt" video. I'm so glad she lived long enough to see it do what it did and get the attention that it got because she did love the "Hurt" video. She was my biggest critic, too. If she didn't like something I did, she told me in a hot minute.

Loder: When one person in a long marriage dies, I would imagine that it is difficult for the surviving spouse to care much about living anymore. But you're still going. Where do you get your resolve and energy?

Cash: She told me when she was in the hospital, "Go to work." I said, "What you talking about?" She said, "Don't worry about me. Go to work." And at the funeral, I could almost hear her saying, "Go to work." Three days after the funeral, everybody said, "You're crazy," but I was in the studio. I stayed in the studio for two weeks, and it was great therapy for me. I think I accomplished more in that couple of weeks than in most of the other years combined.

Loder: And you have plans for another record?

Cash: That's what I started doing, a new record, *American 5*. From New York, I go to California and finish the record with my producer, Rick Rubin. Rick has some more songs and a few things up his sleeve for me that I'm anxious to sit down and listen to and hear what he's got.

Loder: How did you and Rick come to work together?

Cash: I was doing a show in California and when I came offstage, my manager, Lou Robin, said, "There's a man here named Rick Rubin who has a record company and would like to record you." I said, "I don't want to meet him," and he said, "But I think you might like him." I said, "Why?" And he said, "Well, he's different. He's not like the rest of them." So I told him, "Bring him back," and here comes Rick, and immediately I liked him. I said, "If you had me on your record label, what would you do that nobody else has done?" And he said, "What I would do is let you sit down before a microphone with your guitar and sing every song you want to record, just you and your guitar." I said, "You're talking about a dream I had a long time ago to do an album called *Late and Alone*. He said, "That's it. That's the kind of record we want to make." Well, that was my first American Recordings record: just me and my guitar.

Loder: Did Rick tell you that you'd have to make videos, too?

Cash: No, he didn't. Actually, I kind of expected it, and I guess I kind of hoped I would. I've done a lot of videos.

Loder: Do you enjoy making videos?

Cash: Aw, it's OK. Yeah, I enjoy doing videos.

Loder: Kid Rock, Bono of U2—you have many fans among younger musicians. Have you met them? Do they write to you or call?

Cash: I talk to Bono quite often. I've never met Kid Rock. I hope . . . I think I might meet him this weekend. Since June's death, I've hung kind of close to home. I did hear that Kid Rock, through Hank Williams, Jr., wanted to meet me. I still like Emmylou Harris; she's one of my favorites.

Loder: You were there at the beginning of rock & roll music. Do you keep in touch with Jerry Lee Lewis or any of those people?

Cash: I haven't heard from the Killer in quite a while. I get an invitation to his birthday party every year. I understand he's doing well. I'm glad to hear that. I love the Killer; we're good friends.

Loder: Do you remember touring with those people?

Cash: Oh, yeah. I toured with him. There was a package of myself, Jerry Lee, Roy Orbison and Carl Perkins. We toured all over the United States and Canada

Loder: You were all young and wild.

Cash: Oh, yes. Oh, yes we were. We were young and wild and crazy.

Loder: How crazy were you?

Cash: As crazy as you can get. I mean crazy crazy. About the time we were doing these tours, we discovered amphetamines, or I did.

And Jerry, he thought he was going to hell for not preaching. He had gone to a seminary to be a preacher, but he turned to rock & roll. He went on a tangent one night backstage and told us all we were going to hell for singing the kind of music we were singing. I said, "Maybe you're right, Killer, maybe you are."

Loder: Did you feel bad about singing that kind of music?

Cash: Naw, I felt good about it. I felt good about singing what I sang. I never once had a ping of guilt about singing anything that I sang. If I knew I was going to, I wouldn't sing it.

Loder: Do you think of yourself as country or rock & roll or folk?

Cash: I don't think of myself as anything. You have to call me the way you see me—I don't care.

Loder: You recorded "Redemption Song" recently with Joe Strummer. Did you enjoy working with him?

Cash: Oh, he was wonderful. I'm so sad about his death. He was such a nice, sweet guy. [Strummer died on December 29, 2002.]

Loder: How much has record-making changed over the years? Is it out of control now?

Cash: Oh, no; it's easier. With all the new technology, it's great . . . with the Pro Tools and all that.

Loder: Do you feel like you're a monument of American music or that you're just John Cash?

Cash: Just John Cash.

Loder: You must know how people feel about you. Do you get a lot of fan mail?

Cash: Yeah, quite often I hear from my fans. Look, I appreciate all that, all the praise and the glory, but it doesn't change the way I feel about anything, really. I just do what I do and hope the people enjoy it, and just try to be myself in whatever I do.

Loder: Thanks for doing this. One last thing: People that have no faith probably are afraid of death. As someone who has faith, are you able to say to yourself, "My life may end, but it's been good; I'm not afraid?"

Cash: I expect my life to end pretty soon. You know, I'm 71 years old. I have great faith. I have unshakable faith. I've never been angry with God. I've never turned my back on God, so to speak. I never thought that God wasn't there. See, he's my counselor. He's my wisdom. All the good things in my life come from him.

Loder: Where do you think we go after death?

Cash: Well, we all hope to go to heaven.

From 1969 to 1971, "The Johnny Cash Show" ran in prime time on ABC-TV.
The show, taped at Nashville's Ryman Auditorium, featured an eclectic mix
of guest musicians. Bob Dylan (shown leaning on a piano on the opposite page),
Joni Mitchell, Joan Baez, the Monkees, Louis Armstrong, Pete Seeger,
Graham Nash and Merle Haggard, among others, performed on the show.
Johnny also discussed social issues and other topics of the day. The popular
show gained the cover of *TV Guide* on several occasions, and Columbia
Records produced a live album that included Johnny's first recording of
"Sunday Morning Comin' Down," which became one of his biggest hits.

As Edited

THE JOHNNY CASH SHOW

RECEIVED
JUN - 1969
MYLES HARMON

SHOW #1
(#1-JCS-69)

INTRO BOB DYLAN

(MUSIC: PLAYON)

(APPLAUSE)

JOHN:

THANK YOU VERY

(INTRO TO D

SHOW #1
INTRO TO JONI MITCHELL

(MUSIC: PLAYON)

(APPLAUSE)

JOHN:
THANK YOU VERY MUCH...
LADIES AND GENTLEMEN, IT'S
A KIND OF SPECIAL HONOR FOR
ME TO PRESENT YOU TO MY FIRST
GUEST TONIGHT...A YOUNG LADY
FROM SASKATOON, CANADA, A
SONG-WRITER, POET-SINGER...
GENTLE PERSON...WON'T YOU
WELCOME...MISS JONI MITCHEL

(MUSIC: "BOTH SIDES N

(APPLAUSE)

John

TV quickie-movies: A candid appra
By Judith C

TV GUIDE
Local Programs August 30–Sept 5
15¢

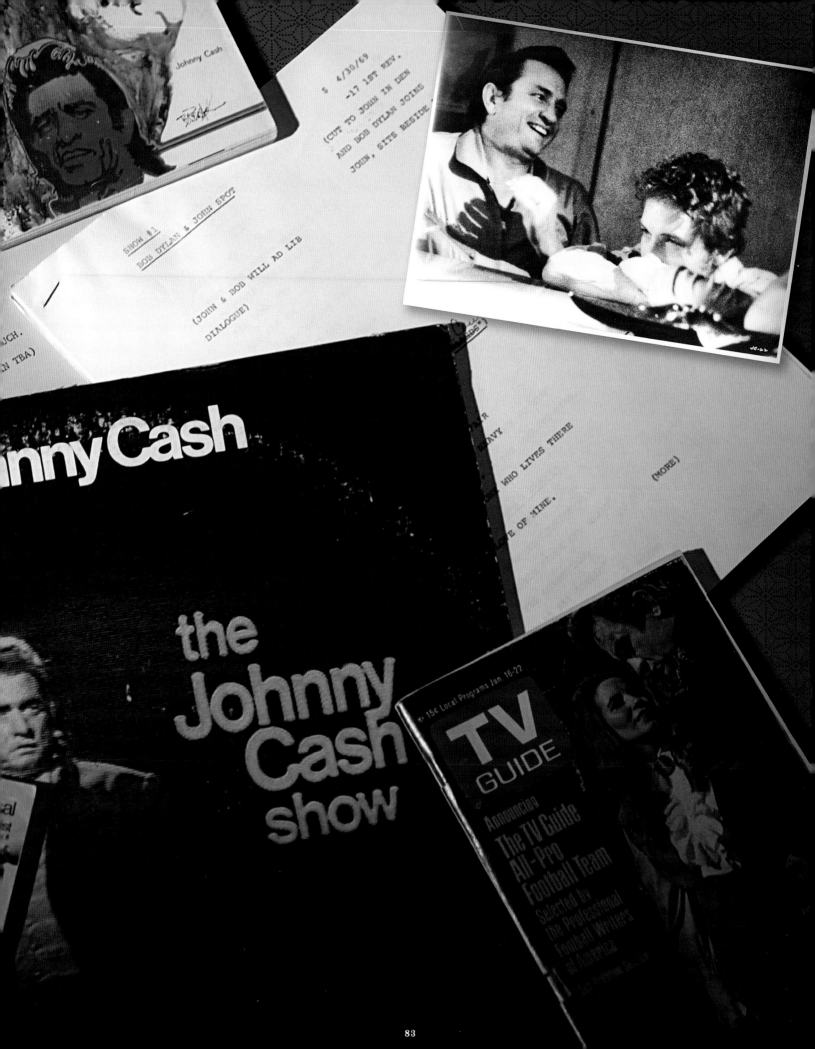

LL-2 Rev. 4-61

STANDARD AFTRA ENGAGEMENT CONTRACT—NETWORK TELEVISION

Single Broadcast or Multiple Broadcasts

Within One Calendar Week

Dated: **JUNE 1** 196 **4**

State of ....

Between   **NEW YORK**

JOHNNY CASH
Box 44
Casita Springs, Colorado   } hereinafter called "Performer,"

and

NATIONAL BROADCASTING COMPANY, INC., 30 Rockefeller Plaza, New York 20, N. Y., hereinafter called "Producer."

Performer shall render artistic services in connection with the rehearsal and broadcast of·the program(s) designated below and preparation in connection with the part or parts to be played:

TITLE OF PROGRAM: .... **TONIGHT** ....

TYPE OF PROGRAM:.......... Sustaining ( ) Commercial **X** Closed Circuit ( )

SPONSOR (if commercial) : .... **VARIOUS** ....

Number of Guaranteed Days of Employment (if Par. 19 of AFTRA TV Network Code is applicable) ....

PLACE OF PERFORMANCE.*.......... **NBC** ....

SCHEDULED FINAL PERFORMANCE DAY .... **JUNE 1, 1964** ....

AFTRA CLASSIFICATION: .... **PERFORMER** ....

PART(S) TO BE PLAYED:..........

COMPENSATION : .... **$320.00** ....

MAXIMUM Rehearsal Hours Included in Above Compensation (if Par. 56(b) of the AFTRA Network TV Code is applicable) ....

Execution of this agreement signifies acceptance by Producer and Performer of all of the above terms and conditions and those on the reverse hereof and attached hereto, if any.

Johnny Cash

Performer   NATIONAL BROADCASTING COMPANY, INC.

                                                                    W Cosmos

Telephone Number   By J. Scibetta/W. Cosmas

Social Security Number

Check to be made payable to.......... **Johnny Cash** ....

*Subject to change in accordance with AFTRA code.

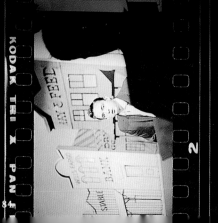

Johnny was paid $320 for his June 1964 appearance on the *Tonight Show* with Johnny Carson. He was the guest host of *Saturday Night Live* on April 17, 1982.

JOHNNY CASH
PRISON BLUES

Young man sittin on the witness stand
Man with a book says raise your hand
Repeat after me, I solemnly swear
Judge looks down at his long hair

And although the young man solemnly swore
Nobody wanted to hear anymore
And it really didn't matter whether truth was there
It was the cut of his clothes
And the length of his hair

And the lonely voice of youth cries what is truth

Young girl dancing to the latest beat
Has found new ways to move her feet
Young man speaking in the city square
Is trying to tell someone he cares

Those girls and boys you are calling wild
Are gonna be the leaders in a little while
New worlds waking to a new born day
And I solemnly swear it'll be their way

Better help that voice of youth
Find what is truth

Johnny was a spokesman for the downtrodden, the poor, the disenfranchised and the underdog. When Bob Dylan came under fire in the early 1960s for his protest songs, Johnny placed an ad in several trade magazines in support of Dylan that carried this message: "Shut Up and Let Him Sing." In 1970, Johnny released "What Is Truth," a song that suggested that society listen to the voice of a new generation.

COMPASSION

※

"We're all the same in the eyes of the Lord."

JRC

The old man slumped against a crutch on the side of the road. He had been walking—hopping, really—as only a man can on one good leg and half of another. He rested standing up, trying to ease the pain from his laborious effort.

A car pulled over and the passenger in the front seat rolled down the window.

"Hey, what are you doing?" he asked.

"I'm in town to get fitted for a prosthetic leg tomorrow," said the old man.

"Where are you staying?"

"I don't have a place to stay, just have to be up at the hospital by morning."

"Come on over here; we'll give you a ride," said the man in the car. The man in the car looked familiar, but the old man couldn't place him. The ride through Nashville took only a few minutes.

The car stopped in front of a hotel. The man in the front seat eased out, opened the back door and helped the old man onto the sidewalk. The old man peered intently at the man helping him.

The man went to the hotel's front desk, checked the old man into a room, and said, "There will be a car here to pick you up and take you to the hospital in the morning. Now have a good night."

As the man walked away, it suddenly became clear to the old man: That was Johnny Cash.

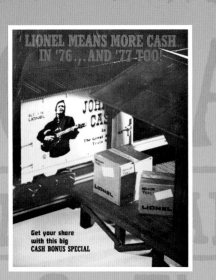

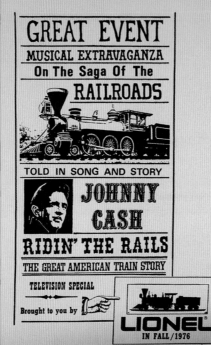

GREAT EVENT
MUSICAL EXTRAVAGANZA
On The Saga Of The
RAILROADS

TOLD IN SONG AND STORY

JOHNNY
CASH

RIDIN' THE RAILS
THE GREAT AMERICAN TRAIN STORY

TELEVISION SPECIAL

Brought to you by ☞ LIONEL
IN FALL/1976

Over➜

Johnny's fascination with trains gained
him an endorsement deal with Lionel in
the 1970s. He appeared in television
commercials and print ads, and on posters,
on behalf of the toy trains company. In 1975,
Lionel sponsored the TV documentary *Ridin' the
Rails* with Johnny as the host, taking viewers on
a tour of railroad history. Johnny followed his own
counsel when it came to endorsements with money
never the primary consideration. If he could help a
friend, then Johnny was likely to honor the request.
Like everything else, Johnny had to "feel" it
before he would agree to a product tie-in.

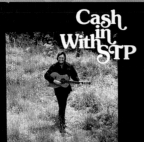

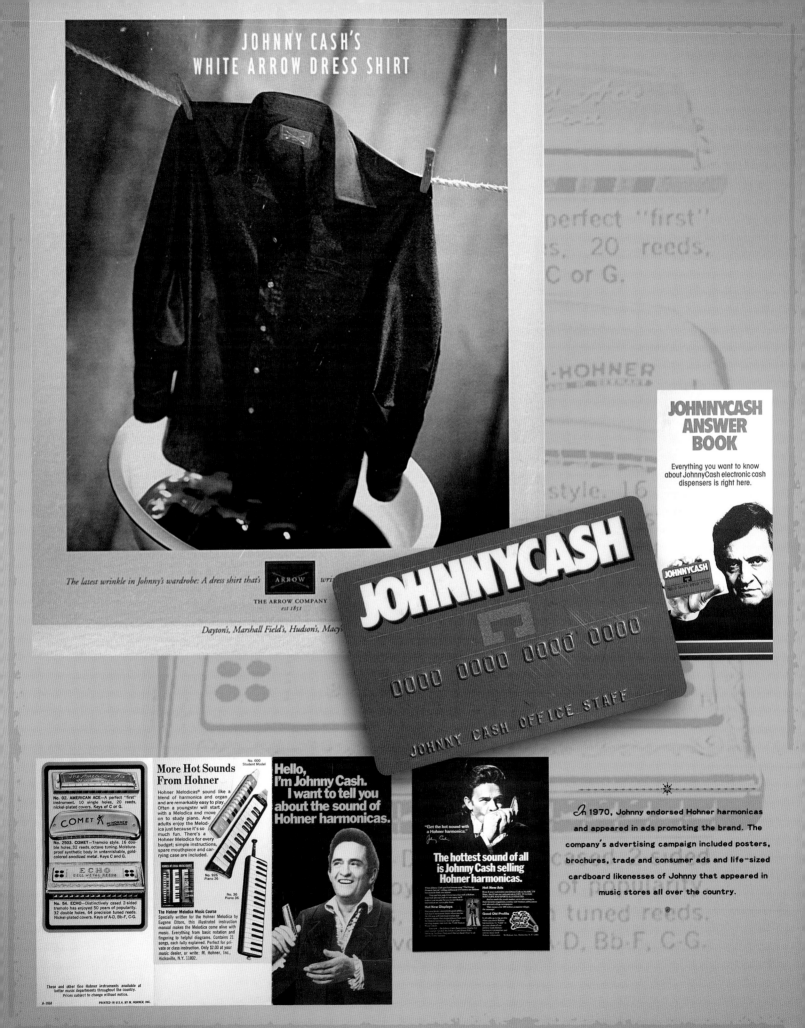

JOHNNY CASH'S
WHITE ARROW DRESS SHIRT

The latest wrinkle in Johnny's wardrobe: A dress shirt that's   wr

ARROW

THE ARROW COMPANY
est 1851

Dayton's, Marshall Field's, Hudson's, Macy's

JOHNNYCASH
ANSWER
BOOK

Everything you want to know
about JohnnyCash electronic cash
dispensers is right here.

JOHNNYCASH

JOHNNYCASH

0000 0000 0000 0000

JOHNNY CASH OFFICE STAFF

No. 600
Student Model

More Hot Sounds From Hohner

No. 02. AMERICAN ACE—A perfect "first"
instrument. 10 single holes, 20 reeds,
nickel-plated covers. Keys of C or G.

COMET

No. 2503. COMET—Tremolo style. 16 double holes, 32 reeds, octave tuning. Moisture-
proof synthetic body in untarnishable, gold-
colored anodized metal. Keys C and G.

ECHO

No. 54. ECHO—Distinctively cased. 2-sided
tremolo has enjoyed 50 years of popularity.
32 double holes, 64 precision tuned reeds.
Nickel-plated covers. Keys of A-D, Bb-F, C-G.

Hohner Melodicas® sound like a
blend of harmonica and organ
and are remarkably easy to play.
Often a youngster will start
with a Melodica and move
on to study piano. And
adults enjoy the Melod-
ica just because it's so
much fun. There's a
Hohner Melodica for every
budget; simple instructions,
spare mouthpiece and car-
rying case are included.

No. 926
Piano 26

No. 36
Piano 36

The Hohner Melodica Music Course
Specially written for the Hohner Melodica by
Eugene Ettore, this illustrated instruction
manual makes the Melodica come alive with
music. Everything from basic notation and
fingering to helpful diagrams. Contains 21
songs, each fully explained. Perfect for private or class instruction. Only $2.00 at your
music dealer, or write: M. Hohner, Inc.,
Hicksville, N.Y. 11802.

These and other fine Hohner instruments available at
better music departments throughout the country.
Prices subject to change without notice.

A-1068   PRINTED IN U.S.A. BY M. HOHNER, INC.

Hello,
I'm Johnny Cash.
I want to tell you
about the sound of
Hohner harmonicas.

"Get the hot sound with
a Hohner harmonica."

The hottest sound of all
is Johnny Cash selling
Hohner harmonicas.

In 1970, Johnny endorsed Hohner harmonicas
and appeared in ads promoting the brand. The
company's advertising campaign included posters,
brochures, trade and consumer ads and life-sized
cardboard likenesses of Johnny that appeared in
music stores all over the country.

Johnny's popularity created a market for any number of collectibles that bore his name and/or likeness. The Franklin Mint plate that features Johnny with his guitar includes a small device that plays the opening line of his hit song, "Man in Black."

Johnny's image appeared on Slurpee cups in 7-Eleven convenience stores in the late 1970s, a testament to his far-reaching appeal. When I told Johnny that I had acquired one for my collection, he grinned devilishly, rolled his eyes and said, "You know you've made it when you're on a Slurpee cup."

Johnny was so popular that concert promoters often tried to book him for multiple performances at a site. This contract, providing for seven performances, covered a five-day period in September 1974, at the Circle Star Theater in San Carlos, California. Johnny's fee was a guarantee of $100,000, plus 65 percent of the ticket sales after $135,000—a princely sum at the time. Ticket prices ranged from $5.50 to $8.50.

PAYROLL
CHECK

S 07 3
SED
87-4

3/31 1974

DOLLARS $ 493.04

HOUSE OF CASH, INC.

John R Cash

AL BANK
NESSEE

1 996 5

"0000049704"

ROSE HALL, HOLIDAY INN BRANCH • MONTEGO BAY, JAMAICA

OF *Barrettown ... Church* $ 200.

Two Hundred and 00

THE BANK OF NOVA SCOTIA
JAMAICA LIMITED
20 DEC 1974
TELLER 1st.
ACCOUNT 1st.
NUMBER
HOLIDAY INN, ROSEHALL JA.

John R Cash
Cash Cash

ENDORSEMENT THIS CHECK WHEN PAID IS ACCEPTED
IN FULL PAYMENT OF THE FOLLOWING ACCOUNT

DATE   AMOUNT
☐ NSF
☐ UNCOLL
☐ FUNDS
☐ ACCT.
CLOSED

IF INCORRECT PLEASE RETURN, NO RECEIPT NECESSARY

JOHNNY CASH TRAILER RANCHO
11195 VENTURA AVENUE
OJAI, CALIFORNIA   93023

☐ SIG.

PAY TO THE
ORDER OF *K Ven ...*

Thirty ...

OAK VIEW BRANCH
CHANNEL ISLANDS
STATE BANK
485 VENTURA AVENUE
OAK VIEW, CALIFORNIA 93022

*For Advertising Trailer Court
on Radio*

1222 1367

DELUXE CHECK PRINTERS - HV

UNE CASH FAN CLUB

STATES OF AMERICA $1000

1110 West Hartman Road
Anderson, Indiana 46011

ONE 7

Phone (317) 644-5466

1971

$ 1000

THOUSAND

JOHNNY CASH

John Cash

NUDIE'S ROD... $ 209.39

Two Hundred Nine and 39/100

JOHNNY CASH ENTERPRISES

URITY FIRST NATIONAL BANK
T MAIN STREET, VENTURA, CALIFORNIA

Johnny Cash

1222 1177 083 009 019

ENDORSEMENT THIS CHECK WHEN PAID IS ACCEPTED
FULL PAYMENT OF THE FOLLOWING ACCOUNT

DATE   AMOUNT
            170 00
FICA   7 14
W.H.   10 70

            152 16

IF INCORRECT PLEASE RETURN, NO RECEIPT NECESSARY

OAK VIEW BRANCH
CHANNEL ISLANDS
STATE BANK
485 VENTURA AVENUE
OAK VIEW, CALIFORNIA 93022

16

JOHNNY CASH TRAILER RANCHO   103
11195 VENTURA AVENUE
OJAI, CALIFORNIA   93023

                    1-3- 1966   90-1367
                                  1222

PAY TO THE
ORDER OF *Carrie L. Cash* $ 152-16

One fifty two 16/100   DOLLARS

JOHNNY CASH TRAILER RANCHO

Mrs John Cash

Johnny Cash

1222 1367

DELUXE CHECK PRINTERS - HV

RAL RESE

ED STATES

VATE

E JOHNNY CASH

STUDIO CITY, CALIFORNIA

LO MAXIMO EN SUSPENSO
LOS CINCO MINUTOS EN QUE HABIA
QUE MATAR—O MORIR...

JOHNNY CASH
DONALD WOODS
CAY FORESTER
PAMELA MASON

5 minutos de Vida
Five minutes to Live

DIST. POR:
PELICULAS AGRASANCHEZ, S.A.
TABASCO 218—MEXICO, D.F.

Johnny's first movie role was playing Johnny Cabot, a psychopathic killer, in *Five Minutes to Live*, released in 1960. Johnny contributed $20,000 halfway through production to keep the low-budget project alive. The film received less than favorable reviews, and it was rereleased as *Door-to-Door Maniac*, again without critical acclaim. Johnny said later, "It was the worst thing I've ever done," and that he regretted taking the role. Vic Tayback, who later gained fame as Mel the diner owner in the TV series *Alice*, and Ron Howard also were in the film. Johnny used Howard as a human shield against the cops in the film's final scenes. Johnny's character died, and Howard's character was reunited with his parents.

IT COULD BE
YOUR STREET...
YOUR HOUSE...
YOUR LIFE!

WHEN THE BELL RINGS...
DON'T ANSWER!

IT COULD BE THE
DOOR-TO-DOOR MANIAC!

JOHNNY CASH · DONALD WOODS · CAY FORESTER · PAMELA MASON · RONNIE HOWARD

COPYRIGHT © 1966 AMERICAN INTERNATIONAL PICTURES
All Rights Reserved Printed in U.S.A.

Five

STARRING JOHNNY
CASH · WOO

DONAL

CO-STARRING
MIDGE WARE · VIC TAYBACK

Screenplay by CAY FORESTER · Produced by JAM

A WOMAN'S PRICE DROPS FAST AS THE TIME LIMIT TICKS AWAY!

How could she extend the moments he had given her!

minutes to Live

CAY S·FORESTER · PAMELA MASON

Introducing Johnny Cash, America's top recording star, as a lusty, romantic, guitar singing powerhouse.

ONNIE HOWARD · Executive Producer LUDLOW FLOWER

LSWORTH · Directed by BILL KARN · Released by SUTTON PICTURES CORP.

Johnny's first starring role in a major motion picture was opposite Kirk Douglas in 1971's *A Gunfight*. Johnny played an aging gunfighter looking to generate income. The plot pitted Douglas and Cash against one another in a public duel for money, winner take all. Johnny turned in an admirable performance, but the film's surreal ending didn't clearly establish who won the duel.

THE PARAMOUNT FILM FESTIVAL PRES

JOHNNY CASH:

PREMIERE OF THE ACCLAIMED DOCUMENTARY

Club Tram #55 -William St. City

THE PARAMOUNT
CINEMA - CLUB
43 MELVILLE RD.
WEST BRUNSWICK

Your host is Bob 'The Brakeman' Eagle
— "Hear that lonesome whistle blow!"

NASHVIL
POLICE DE

Johnny's deep Christian faith led to the making of *The Gospel Road* in 1971, after he had a dream that he was standing atop Mount Sinai in Israel, reading from the Bible. That dream became the opening scene in the film, which was funded by Johnny and June's $500,000. Johnny served as the on-camera narrator, and the director, Robert Elfstrom, played the role of Jesus. June played Mary Magdalene, and the rest of the cast was comprised of friends, family and native Israelis. *The Gospel Road*, the first film shot in its entirety in the Holy Land, told the story of Christ visually and musically. After the movie had run its course in theaters, Johnny gave it to his friend Billy Graham, who showed it in spiritual gatherings around the world. In 1973, Columbia Records released a double album that included songs from the movie; several made the best-selling charts as singles. Johnny said that *The Gospel Road* was among his most satisfying accomplishments.

Johnny **Cash** in person

for the L.A.-Orange County Premiere of

THE GOSPEL ROAD

20th CENTURY FOX

Benefit Performance for Youth for Christ/Campus Life

JOHN WAYNE THEATRE, KNOTTS BERRY FARM

WEDNESDAY, MAY 8th, 1974, 8:00 p.m.

This ticket entitles you to attend a reception honoring
the Cash family. 7 p.m. at the Le Baron Hotel.

"I'M JUST TRYING TO BE A GOOD CHRISTIAN.
YOU KNOW, THERE ARE DIFFERENT KINDS OF CHRISTIANS.
THERE'S PREACHING CHRISTIANS, CHURCH-PLAYING CHRISTIANS, AND
THERE'S PRACTICING CHRISTIANS—
AND I'M TRYING VERY HARD
TO BE A PRACTICING CHRISTIAN.
IF YOU TAKE THE WORDS OF JESUS LITERALLY
AND APPLY THEM TO YOUR
EVERYDAY LIFE, YOU DISCOVER THAT THE
GREATEST FULFILLMENT
YOU'LL EVER FIND REALLY DOES LIE IN
GIVING."

JOHNNY CASH

Johnny's creativity extended beyond his music. In addition to being a serious photographer, he frequently sketched. The drawing on the opposite page, entitled *Shroud*, is Johnny's interpretation of the Shroud of Turin, which is believed to have been the linen cloth placed over the face of Jesus Christ before he was entombed. Johnny used a pencil to cover a sheet of sketch paper with lead and then created Christ's image with an eraser. Concerned how others would view the drawing, he elicited my opinion. I told him that it was a magnificent piece of work, and he said, "Well, if you like it, I want you to keep the original. But would you have some copies made for me to give to June and my kids for Christmas?" I had 10 copies made and fixed on matting, and I sent them to Johnny in time for the holidays.

❈

ACTS SPIRITUAL   — CHAPTER 23

I. NAME: NAMES:

Forty Fasting Fanatics   FASTING FANATICS

                             IL AND CONSPIRACY

                     ONE NAME, WRITE IT

                     PACE PROVIDED AND

                      IT.)

II. KEY VERSE: SUGGESTED KEY VERSE:

Ac. 23.11 And the night following, the Lord stood by him and said, "Be of good cheer Paul for as thou hast testified of me in Jerusalem, so must thou beard witness also at Rome.

1. ACTS 23:11
(WRITE THE VERSE IN THE SPACE PROVIDED AND MEMORIZE IT.)

III. OUTLINE:

❈

Johnny carried a Bible with him and used it as a reference book for the spiritual songs he wrote. In the 1970s, he decided to formalize his Bible study and enrolled in an extensive correspondence course at Southwest International University. The school mailed study courses and tests to Johnny, and after he returned the completed tests, the process was repeated until he had fulfilled the requirements for a doctorate in Bible study. Johnny gave me binders that held hundreds of pages of his handwritten tests, essays and study reports. The depth and scope of the work, and the stellar grades he received, reflected his dedication to expanding his faith.

IV. PLACE: *Temple, Jerusalem*   (LIST THE PLACE OR PLACES
Rome. Caesarea. Antipatris, Cilicia. MENTIONED IN THIS CHAPTER)

AYER UNCEASING" OF THE FACULTY OF SOUTH...

SPIRITUAL VALUE WHICH MAY BE OBTAINED FROM THIS

INCENTIVE FOR A MORE ACTIVE PARTICIPATION IN SOUT...

LINK THE SOULS OF MANKIND TO CHRIST JESUS FOR ETERN...

THE PEACE AND SECURITY WHICH COMES TO ANY INDIV...

E SALVATION OFFERED THROUGH CHRIST'S...

AND SECURITY WHICH PASSETH

---

chapters 20-2

IV & V

GOSPELS II -- CHRIST OF

PART IV -- FOUR

SPEC

CHAPTER 20: THE TRANSFIGU

I. PAGE 313-314: ACCOR

DID THE TRANSFIGURAT

II. PAGE 314: WHO DID JE

James & Joh...

the most

III.

(A)

Gospels II

1975

...d out materials + discuss · Assign

...d Ch. 20 + do p. 1+2 in Workbook.

1975

...o · Ch. 21 in C...

Discuss · Assig... Cash, John

Assignment: —

10, 1975

Discuss Ass

Assignment

...arch 17, 1975

Discuss

Assignmen...

March 24, 1975

Discu...

Assig...

March 31st

D...

Gospels II

1. Content Questions (515)

2. Time Chart (10)

3. Question X chapter 23 (10)
   Question XI chapter 23

4. Question X chapter 30 (10)

5. Question XI chapter 32 (10)

6. Question X chapter 34 (10)

7. Question XVI chapter 34 (10)

	points
515	515
10	10
10	10
10	10
10	10
10	10
10	10
10	

(585) 585

Excellent

585—526

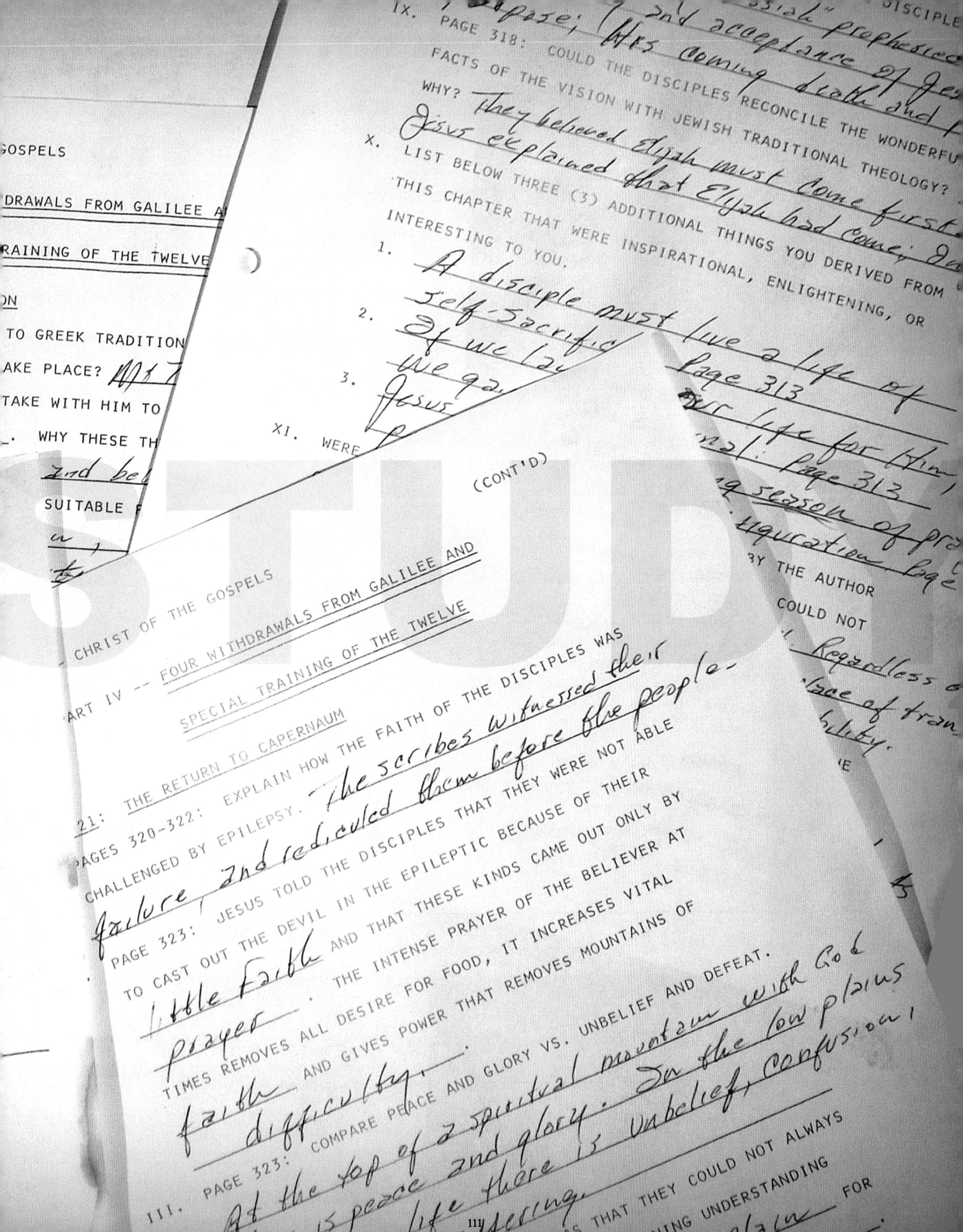

GOSPELS

DRAWALS FROM GALILEE A

RAINING OF THE TWELVE

ON

TO GREEK TRADITION

AKE PLACE? *handwritten*

TAKE WITH HIM TO

. WHY THESE TH

handwritten 2nd be

SUITABLE F

IX. ...pose; ...2nd acceptance of Je...
PAGE 318: COULD THE DISCIPLES RECONCILE THE WONDERFU...
FACTS OF THE VISION WITH JEWISH TRADITIONAL THEOLOGY?
WHY? *handwritten* They believed Elijah must come first.
X. *handwritten* Jesus explained that Elijah had come. Ja...
LIST BELOW THREE (3) ADDITIONAL THINGS YOU DERIVED FROM
THIS CHAPTER THAT WERE INSPIRATIONAL, ENLIGHTENING, OR
INTERESTING TO YOU.

1. *handwritten* A disciple must live a life of   Page 313
2. *handwritten* Self-Sacrific...   ...r life for him,...   Page 313
3. *handwritten* If we lay...   ...nal...
   handwritten We ga...   ...ng season of pro...
   handwritten Jesus...   ...guration... Page...

XI. WERE   BY THE AUTHOR
COULD NOT
handwritten Regardless of
...lace of tran...
...bility.

CHRIST OF THE GOSPELS

ART IV -- FOUR WITHDRAWALS FROM GALILEE AND
SPECIAL TRAINING OF THE TWELVE

THE RETURN TO CAPERNAUM

(CONT'D)

21: PAGES 320-322: EXPLAIN HOW THE FAITH OF THE DISCIPLES WAS
CHALLENGED BY EPILEPSY. *handwritten* The scribes witnessed their
handwritten failure 2nd rediculed them before the people.

PAGE 323: JESUS TOLD THE DISCIPLES THAT THEY WERE NOT ABLE
TO CAST OUT THE DEVIL IN THE EPILEPTIC BECAUSE OF THEIR
handwritten little faith   AND THAT THESE KINDS CAME OUT ONLY BY
handwritten prayer   . THE INTENSE PRAYER OF THE BELIEVER AT
TIMES REMOVES ALL DESIRE FOR FOOD, IT INCREASES VITAL
handwritten faith   AND GIVES POWER THAT REMOVES MOUNTAINS OF
handwritten difficulty   .

III. PAGE 323: COMPARE PEACE AND GLORY VS. UNBELIEF AND DEFEAT.
handwritten At the top of a spiritual mountain with God
handwritten ...ce is peace 2nd glory. In the low plains
handwritten ...life there is unbelief, confusion,
WAS THAT THEY COULD NOT ALWAYS
...ining understanding FOR

The Wanderlust

I went a wandering down streets paved with gold
lifted some stones
saw the skin and bones
of a city without a soul
I went out wandering under an atomic sky
where the ground won't turn
and the rain it burns
like the tears when ~~you~~ said goodbye

Chorus
Yeah I went with nothing
but the thought that you'd be there too
looking for you........
WA WA WA WA WANDERING'

I went a wandering through the capitals of tin
where men can't walk
or freely talk
and sons turn their fathers in
I stopped outside a church house
where citizens like to sit
they say they want the kingdom
but they dont want God in it

Chorus
I went out with nothing
but the thought you'd be there too
looking for you
wa wa wa wa wandering

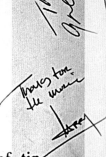

In February 1993, U2 lead singer Bono learned that his hero, Johnny Cash, would be performing in Dublin, Ireland. Bono quickly wrote "The Wanderlust," in hopes that he could get Johnny to record the song with U2. Bono reached Johnny the day before the Dublin concert and convinced him to do the song.

I went out walking, to places not yet named
where   people dreamed instead of schemed
and no one was ashamed
I went a wandering, down that ol' eight lane
I passed by - a thousand signs
looking for my own name

Chorus
I went out with nothing
but the thought you'd be there too
looking for you
wa wa wa wa wandering

I went out walking, down that widening road
where no ones trusting no one
and concience a too heavy load
I went a wandering   where glass cities stand
concrete skies, I passed them by
as they turned back into sand
I went a walking in search of experience
to taste and touch to feel as much
as a man before he repents

Chorus
I went out with nothing
but the thought you'd be there too
looking for you
wa wa wa wa wandering

The song was recorded on the afternoon of February 8, and U2 joined Johnny onstage at his concert (background photo) that evening. These are the sheets used by Johnny during the recording, with his handwritten changes. At the end of the session, each member of U2 signed the first page of the lyrics and presented the sheets to Johnny. The song title was changed to "The Wanderer," and the tune was a solo cut on U2's *Zooropa* album.

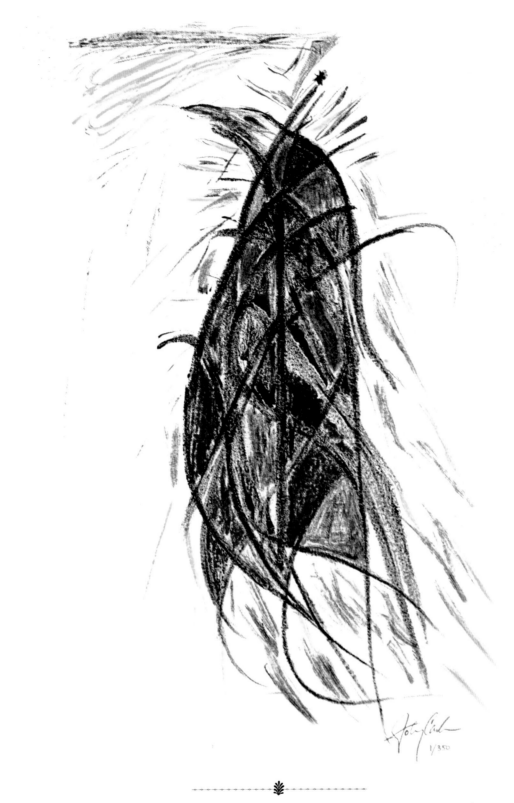

John Cash
1/350

The only piece of published Johnny Cash art is entitled *Flight*. I was so overwhelmed when I first saw *Flight*, one of Johnny's first paintings on canvas, that I wanted to make serigraphs of it. "People would want to own my painting?" he asked humbly. In July 1996, Johnny signed 300 serigraphs of the painting. I showed *Flight* to several high-profile art dealers in Los Angeles, and they, too, were taken by it. They wanted to know if Johnny would commit to painting regularly, and suggested that he could become a major celebrity artist whose work would be valued by collectors. Asked about his intentions as a painter, Johnny placed a fist over his heart and said, "You've got to feel it here to be able to paint. I don't think I can commit to a steady supply of them." No one should have expected Johnny to paint for the sake of meeting commercial demand. After all, he never did that with his music.

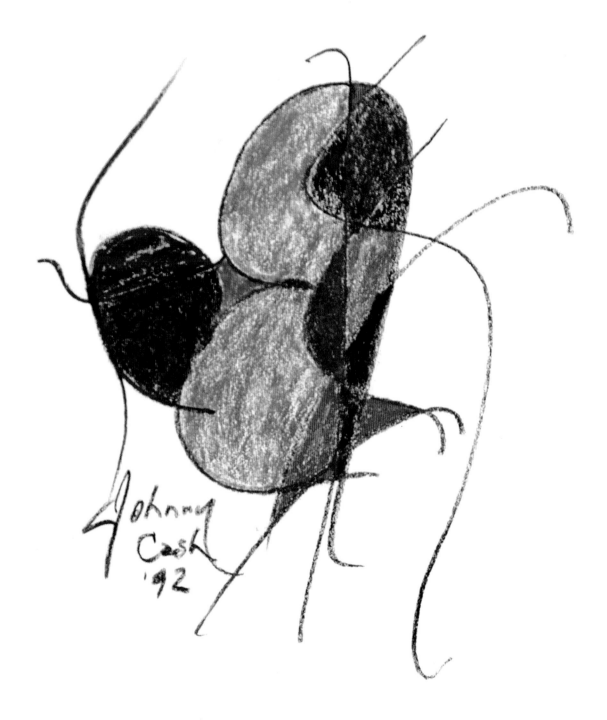

A PERSONAL NOTE

In 1976 I wrote a book, MAN IN BLACK. The purpose of this book was several fold. ~~I suppose~~ one of the primary ~~motives~~ was to re-dedicate myself on a continuous basis ~~and~~ how close I really came to losing it all because of drugs, and ~~also~~ serve as an inspiration to others.

Reasons
and to remind myself
Possibly

My problem in drugs was the prescription kind issued by the physician that serve a legitimate need. I ~~was using them as a crutch~~ ~~and~~ buying them by the hundreds, using every subterfuge in the book to get some doctor to write the prescription.

About than!

I considered my problem person until I was arrested in October 1966 in Lafayette, Georgia. I realized my problem also affected others when Sheriff Ralph Jones expressed his disappointment in me and his long time appreciation of my abilities as an entertainer. As he let me out of jail, he handed me back my pills and said, "Go on and take them and get out of here." His remarks cut to the bone as he related how he and his wife had all my albums of hymns, etc. As I walked out he said, "Do with your life whatever you want to, but remember you've got the free will to either kill yourself or save yourself."

habit-forming medication

Getting off ~~of drugs~~ was not easy. But every friend I had did everything they could to help. I remember Dr. Nat Winston said, "John, I'm a doctor, ~~I'm~~ a psychiatrist, and I've seen a lot of people in the shape you're in. Frankly, I don't think there's much chance for you....get ready for the fight of your life. I'll be back tomorrow night and see how you're doing."

I made the transition to a drug free life. I hope this message and my book, MAN IN BLACK, can be an inspiration to you, as my friends were an inspiration to me to kick the habit. Again, I hope you can see that a drug ~~habit~~ is everyone's problem.

problem

Sincerely,

Johnny Cash

are that person

P.S. If you ~~have that problem~~, or know of someone who ~~has~~, get help -- NOW!!!!!

Johnny fought an addiction to prescription pain-killing drugs for much of his adult life. He sought relief from a jaw injury that was never fully repaired, despite many surgeries, and often caused him excruciating pain. Johnny's drug problem became so acute in late 1983 that he went to the Eisenhower Medical Center in Rancho Mirage, California, for evaluation and was admitted to the Betty Ford Center for treatment. When I visited Johnny at the center shortly before the holidays, I realized that he would be there without family or friends on Christmas, so I sent him a decorated tree. He later told me that the tree was "the talk of the place."

Johnny and I never had any in-depth discussions about his drug usage. In fact, the subject came up only once. I was about to enter an Orange County, California, venue where Johnny was playing a concert when one of his assistants beckoned me to Johnny's tour bus. I was on the steps when Johnny boomed, "Hey, Bill, I'm off dope!" The excitement in his voice so caught me by surprise that I neglected to return his greeting. He looked healthy and vital, and there was an air of freshness about him.

Johnny was candid about his addictions in public forums. He acknowledged that every day was fraught with temptation and that it was a struggle for him to resist. In a world in which many celebrities and their handlers are forthcoming only when it suits their needs, Johnny's raw honesty was always refreshing.

Johnny recounted his life and dedication to Jesus Christ in the Christian comic book, *Hello, I'm Johnny Cash*, published in 1976.

Taos, N.M. June 1970

We drove from Santa Fe to Taos
The black, table top mountains
Climbed up like stair-steps
Toward Taos
The Rio Grande, ran beside the road
Then we topped a last hill,
And on the plateau
The great beautiful plateau
Stretched to our left a hundred mile
The Rio Grande, a million years ago
Cut a deep, wide awesome gorge
Across the plateau
Proud, peaceful, mountains
Look down on Taos
Proud, peaceful, happy people
Breathe the clean Taos air,
The only thing disturbing the countryside
Were giant dust-devils
And they're a thing of beauty

Upon our return from Taos,
Someone had the nerve to remark,
"Taos is overrun with hippies, isn't it."
If that's all you saw at Taos
You've got no business going there.

I heard on the news
That there is a lull in the fighting
In Viet Nam
Because so many Vietnamese
Are busy planting
A rice crop again
The report said
~~b~~ That full scale fighting
Is expected to resume
Immediately after the planting season
I reply;
What kind of animal is Man
That he would pause
In his killing
In order to go about the business
Of preparing for the living
Knowing
That he will immediately return
To the business of ~~the~~ killing.

J.C

*Johnny addressed his life for the first time in his 1975 autobiography,
Man in Black. More than 1.5 million copies of the book were sold, making
it one of the best-selling celebrity autobiographies ever published.
Two decades later, Johnny and Patrick Carr wrote Johnny's
second book, Cash, the Autobiography.*

Johnny Cash
MAN IN BLACK

His own story in his own words

No matter which way you look at him,

JOHNNY CASH

...ner!

A... ...ge and other engagements.

(...AL MGR.) OR PHONE HO 6-3366
HOLLYWOOD, CALIF.

❋

Johnny introduced knee boots to his stage wardrobe
in the mid-1970s. This elaborate pair from the 1980s,
designed by Johnny, features multicolored leather
inlay and an alligator skin foot. It is believed that
the renowned Lucchese Boot Company made this
pair. Johnny's boot size was 13D.

❋

MANY WAYS

...CASH...

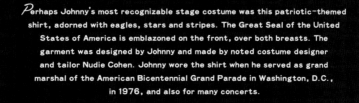

*P*erhaps Johnny's most recognizable stage costume was this patriotic-themed
shirt, adorned with eagles, stars and stripes. The Great Seal of the United
States of America is emblazoned on the front, over both breasts. The
garment was designed by Johnny and made by noted costume designer
and tailor Nudie Cohen. Johnny wore the shirt when he served as grand
marshal of the American Bicentennial Grand Parade in Washington, D.C.,
in 1976, and also for many concerts.

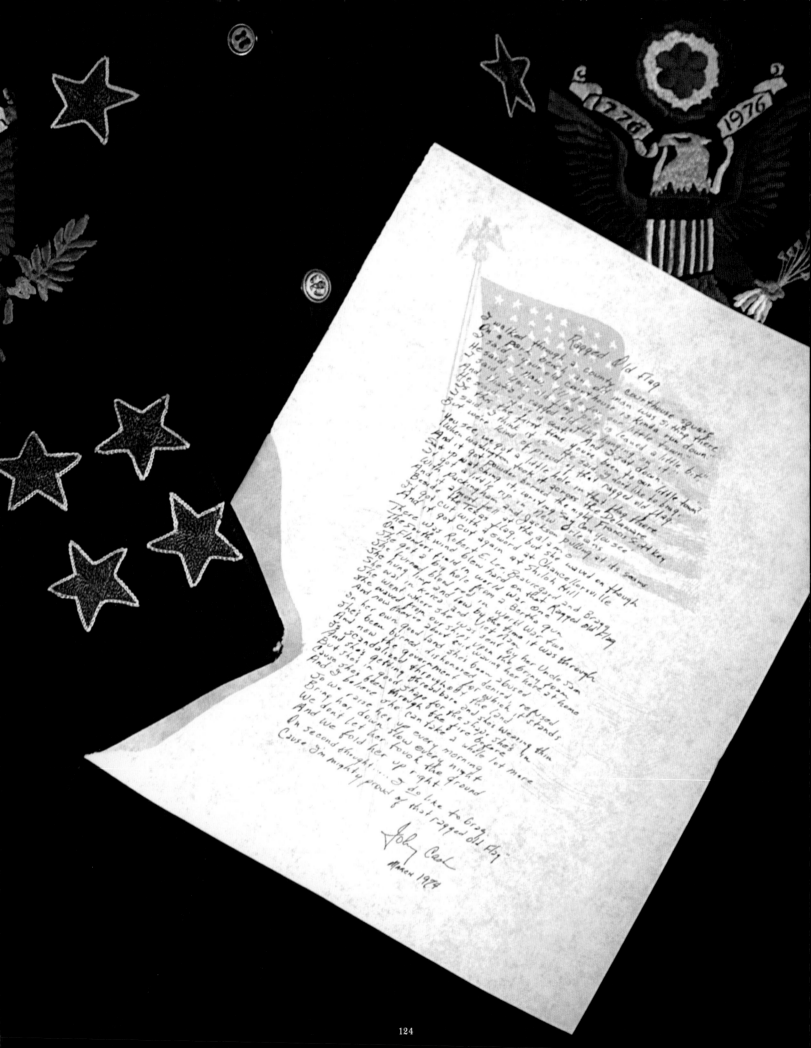

Ragged Old Flag

I walked through a county courthouse square
On a park bench an old man was sitting there
He said "Are you going to look around?"
I said "I guess I am but I don't know"
He said "the old flag pole is kinda run down"
And "that's a ragged old flag you're looking at"
I said "This is the first time I've been to your little town"
He said "Our flag is a ragged old flag"

You see we got a little hole in that flag there
When Washington took it across the Delaware
And it got powder burned the night Francis Scott Key
sat watching it writing "say can you see"
And it got a bad rip in New Orleans
With Packingham and Jackson tugging at its seams
And it almost fell at the Alamo
beside the Texas flag, but she waved on though

She got cut with a sword at Chancellorsville
And she got cut again at Shiloh Hill
There was Robert E. Lee and Beauregard and Bragg
And the south wind blew hard on that Ragged Old Flag
On Flanders field in world war one
She got a big hole from a Bertha gun
She turned blue and bloody red in world war two
She hung limp and low by the time it was through
She was in Korea and Vietnam
She went where she was sent by her Uncle Sam
She waved from our ships upon the briny foam
And now they've about quit waving her back here at home

In her own good land here she's been abused
She's been burned, dishonored, denied and refused
And the government for which it stands
Has scandalized throughout the land
And she's getting threadbare and she's wearing thin
But she's in good shape for the shape she's in
Cause she's been through the fire before
And I believe she can take a whole lot more

So we raise her up every morning
And we bring her down slow every night
We don't let her touch the ground
And we fold her up right
On second thought..... I do like to brag
Cause I'm mighty proud of that ragged old flag

John Cash
March 1974

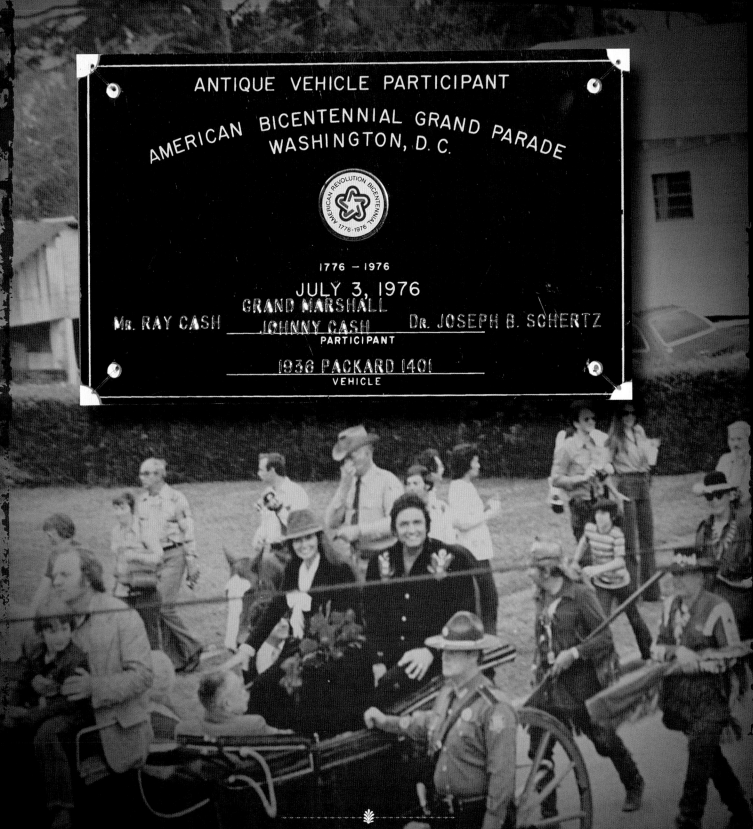

ANTIQUE VEHICLE PARTICIPANT

AMERICAN BICENTENNIAL GRAND PARADE
WASHINGTON, D.C.

1776 – 1976

JULY 3, 1976
GRAND MARSHALL
JOHNNY CASH

Mr. RAY CASH   Dr. JOSEPH B. SCHERTZ
PARTICIPANT

1936 PACKARD 1401
VEHICLE

Johnny was the grand marshal of the American Bicentennial Grand Parade
in Washington, D.C., on July 3, 1976. What pleased Johnny most about
the event was that his father, Ray Cash, a war veteran, rode with
him and June on the parade route. This plaque was affixed to the
antique car that carried the Cashes.

I WALK THE LINE

Johnny called me one day and said he and June were coming to my memorabilia gallery, which was in an outdoor mall in Newport Beach, California. People took notice and stared in awe as the famous man in black jeans and a blue checkered flannel shirt walked into my store, looking happy and relaxed. "I have something for you," said Johnny as he wrote his name and address in the guest register. He reached into the black alligator-skin notebook that he was carrying and pulled out a document. "I heard you wanted these," he said. Two years earlier, Johnny's neice, Kelly Hancock, had asked me if there was anything of Johnny's that I wanted for my collection, and I joked that I would love to have his handwritten lyrics to "I Walk the Line." That's what Johnny took from his notebook and presented to me. He then pulled out a couple of guitar picks and suggested how the pieces might be displayed in a frame. I was so grateful for Johnny's generous gift that I wanted to reciprocate in kind. I knew that he had a deep interest in U.S. presidents, so I decided to put together a collection of presidential signatures for him. As we walked out of my gallery together, I asked Johnny who his favorite president was. "James Garfield," he replied without hesitation. "I wrote a song about him called 'Mr. Garfield.'

Let me sing it for you." And he did.

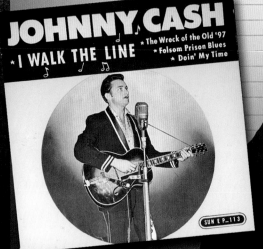

I Walk the Line By John R Cash

I keep a close watch on this heart of mine
I keep my eyes wide open all the time
I keep the ends out for the tie that binds
Because you're mine, I walk the line

As sure as night is dark and day is light
I keep you on my mind both day and night
And happiness I've known proves that it's right
Because you're mine, I walk the line

I find it very very easy to be true
I find myself alone when each days through
Yes I'll admit, that I'm a fool for you
Because you're mine, I walk the line

You've got a way to keep me on your side
You give me cause for love that I can't hide
For you I know I'd even try to turn the tide
Because you're mine, I walk the line

Repeat 1st verse

by
Johnny Cash
@John Cash

Dear Mr. Cash:

Mrs. Nixon and I were delighted to have the opportunity to welcome you and Mrs. Cash to the White House last Friday and I want to express my thanks to you once more for the superb entertainment you provided for all of us who had the privilege of seeing you. The spirit of your music and of your message demands great talent as well as a special kind of integrity. Needless to say, the enthusiastic reception you achieved here proves anew that you possess these and many other gifts in abundance.

I will always be grateful for your kindness and I hope you will convey my appreciation also to the Carter Family, the Statler Brothers and the Tennessee Three, in addition to Carl Perkins, for all they did to make the evening so enjoyable and so very successful.

Mrs. Nixon joins me in sending warm personal regards to Mrs. Cash, to you and to young John Carter.

Sincerely,

Richard Nixon

Mr. John R. Cash
Box 207, Caudill Drive
Hendersonville, Tennessee

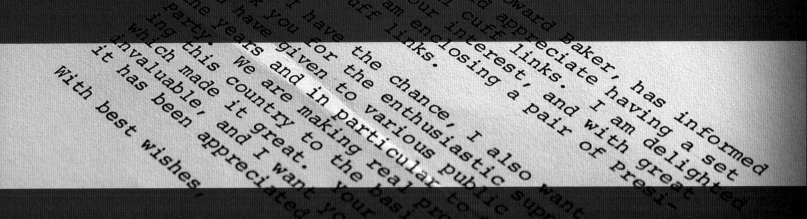

THE WHITE HOUSE
WASHINGTON

July 30, 1983

Dear Johnny:

My good friend, Howard Baker, has informed
me that you would appreciate having a set
of Presidential cuff links. I am delighted
to know of your interest, and with great
pleasure I am enclosing a pair of Presidential cuff links.

Since I have the chance, I also want to
thank you for the enthusiastic support
you have given to various public causes over
the years and in particular to the Republican
Party. We are making real progress in return-
ing this country to the basic principles
which made it great. Your support has been
invaluable, and I want you to know how much
it has been appreciated.

With best wishes,

Sincerely,

Ronald Reagan

THE WHITE HOUSE
WASHINGTON

December 8, 1977

To Johnny Cash

Rosalynn and I so appreciate your efforts in trying
to change your schedule to be with us last night.

It was a wonderful evening and we missed you.

Thank you for being a good and loyal friend.

Sincerely,

Jimmy

Mr. Johnny Cash
Caudill Drive
Hendersonville, Tennessee 37075

Richard Nixon was the first president that Johnny got to know well. At Nixon's invitation,
Johnny and June sang at the White House in 1969. (Johnny also performed for five
other presidents.) These photos were taken at the White House a few years later,
after Johnny spoke to a Senate subcommittee on prison reform.

Haldeman   Nov 11 1974

Erlichman

Mitchell   Mr Wilson

Morn June 23 1972

(Mr Butterfield has last word
on accuracy of this tape)

Motion made that transcript
1A not be evidence.

James Neal rebuffs

Mr. Wilson holds to.

Judge Refuses

Business Concerning Gen.
Watters - Neal retorts.
Judge requests Gov Memoranda
Neal Calls Gen Walters
Jury sits.

Johnny's patriotism was one of the threads in his recording career. His thorough knowledge of American history is evident in many of his songs, as well as concept albums. Whether it was the struggles of the American Indian or the Vietnam War, Johnny provided an insightful and informative voice on controversial topics. In 1974, Johnny's attorney, Jim Neal, joined the legal team investigating the White House's role in Watergate. Johnny attended some of the sessions and took notes (left) on hotel stationary. He once held Richard Nixon in high esteem, but felt betrayed by the president after the Watergate scandal was exposed.

26

J.
this new generation &
Of out youth
Just like the last
Is searching for the truth
And over all these centuries the Word
From st Paul to Billy Graham
Truth is heard
And the preacher said, of truth,
Jesus said

Billy
Graham " I am the Way, the truth and
the light."

It seems that all the World
Is full of greed
there's so much hate
And there is so much need
~~other~~ others show us that they do not care
What should we do when there is no love, there
And the preacher said, Of Love, Jesus
said.

Billy
Graham "- - - - love thy neighbor as thyself.

❋

Johnny and the Reverend Billy Graham first met in the early 1970s and forged a close friendship
that lasted until the end of Johnny's life. Graham initially sought out Johnny, curious about Johnny's
powerful influence over America's youth at the time. The two realized that, although they walked
different paths, they had a lot in common. Each was a Southern Baptist and held a deep faith in
God. Johnny and June appeared at many Billy Graham Crusades. Johnny wrote "The Preacher
Said Jesus Said" for his *Man in Black* album in 1971, and he and Graham recorded the
lyrics—the only time they collaborated on a commercial record.

❋

BILLY GRAHAM
Montreat, N.C. 28757
September 20, 1976

My dear Johnny,

It was a delight to talk to you on the phone
briefly last evening. I am delighted to know
that you like the little message for your
Christmas show.

Whether Ruth and I will be able to spend a
night with you or not is up in the air due
to a heavy schedule around the date of November
5. At the moment we are tentatively planning
to spend the night of November 4 with you, if
that is agreeable. However, I do have to keep
it tentative, and if that is not possible, we
will take a raincheck. I wonder if you can
give me the time of day of the taping. There
is a possibility I will have to fly in and fly
out on that date.

You can tell your people that they can go ahead
and put this on the teleprompter. Hopefully,
I will be able to read it as though I'm not
reading it (because of familiarity with it).

With warmest Christian greetings, I am

                              Cordially yours,

                              Billy

Mr. Johnny Cash
Caudille Drive
Hendersonville, Tn. 37075

133

Gene Autry

5858 SUNSET BOULEVARD · LOS ANGELES · CALIFORNIA 90028

March 17, 1978

Dear Johnny:

I have been advised that you have recorded your song, "Who Was Gene Autry" to be included in your new album, "I Would Like To See You Again".

I am delighted that you want to use the song in the album and you certainly have my permission to do so.

I hope it will be a million seller for you.

With warmest personal regards,

Gene Autry

Gene Autry

Mr. Johnny Cash
c/o Mr. Marty Klein
Agency for the Performing Arts
9000 Sunset Blvd., Suite 315
Los Angeles, CA 90069

Sheriff's Office, Davidson County, Tenn.

FATE THOMAS, Sheriff

By virtue of the power vested in me as Sheriff of Davidson County under the laws of Tennessee, I have this day deputized

John R. Cash

a Deputy Sheriff to execute any and all processes that may come into his hands and to maintain the peace and dignity of the State, and arrest any and all persons violating the Criminal laws of the State of Tennessee.

This Commission may be revoked at my will.

1420

This day of ____ 12th

September ____

____, 19 79

Signed ____

____ Sheriff

Johnny was called an outlaw more than he was called a man of the law. He played lawmen in a couple of movies, but few people know that he was a sworn member of the Davidson County, Tennessee, Sheriff's Office. Johnny and the sheriff were friends. This was his official ID card, which entitled him to all privileges afforded other sworn officers. Johnny said that he never arrested anyone or wrote any tickets.

❊

As a resident of Ventura County, California, in the 1960s, Johnny did little to endear himself to local law enforcement authorities. He was using drugs regularly, and his behavior was often erratic. On one occasion, Johnny took his band to the roof of his home to play Christmas songs for the neighbors. Some neighbors disapproved, and Johnny again incurred the wrath of the Ventura Police Department. A decade later, no longer a resident of the county, Johnny received the badge on the opposite page from the Ventura Police Department in recognition of his "unselfish devotion to youth."

❊

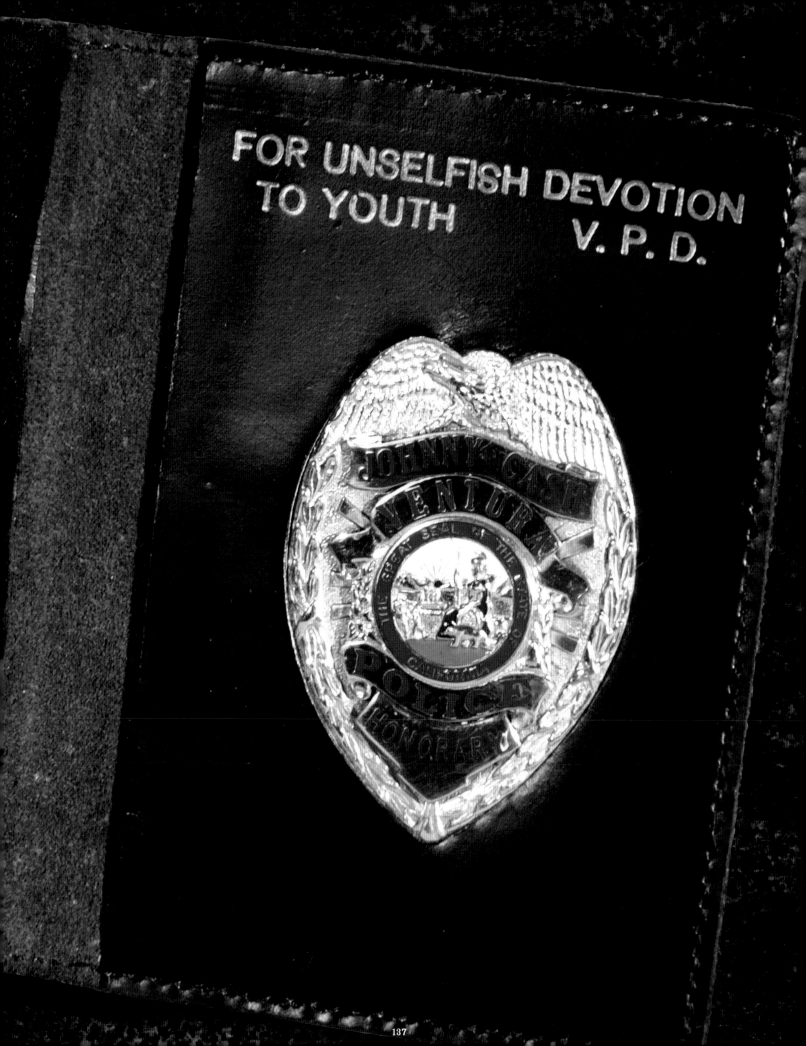

Name **Johnny Cash**

Why do you collect? I'm a history buff. The things I collect touch lives of fascinating people—plus places & events

What do you collect? Autographs of the Presidents of the U.S.— Roman Coins — Ancient Judean Coins Certain 19th Century Firearms — Guitars

When did you start collecting? All my life, different things.

What was the first thing you ever collected? Pretty rocks — Marbles

Which item(s) are your favorite(s)? My McKenney — King Indian Chief Books. Written and painted in 1830's & 40's — Coins from Pontius Pilates time

What is the strangest thing in your collection? A Bronze Roman Spear Point found at the Eastern Wall in Jerusalem. A Cananite lamp

If you had to choose only one item to keep, what would it be? A Black Martin Guitar, the first one made. Made for me in 71. Autographed by Gene Autry.

Is there any item you've searched for but can't find? A George Washington Peace Medal given to Indians Chiefs in late 18th, early 19th C.

Johnny Cash
Signature

Johnny was a collector. He was most interested in items that had historical significance, and I collected things that related to him. We exchanged many items over the years. I would give Johnny a letter written by Abraham Lincoln; he would give me a song that he had handwritten or a guitar that he had used. In the 1990s, I published a magazine called *Pop Culture Collecting*, which Johnny enjoyed reading. I asked him to fill out this form on his collecting interests. He gladly obliged, and I used the material in the magazine.

In 1974, Johnny celebrated his 20th year as an entertainer by commissioning this elaborate belt buckle. Only 100 were made, and he gave them to his family, close friends and business associates. Johnny had belt buckle number 101. It was a surprise gift from his manager, Lou Robin. Johnny's buckle was cast in solid 14 karat gold, and he wore it proudly throughout the 1970s and 1980s.

Over the years, Johnny designed a number of souvenir belt buckles, like this one, which were made available to the fans.

PUBLICITY MATERIAL
from
JOHNNY CASH

15445 VENTURA BOULEVARD
SHERMAN OAKS, CALIFORNIA

JOHNNY CASH FAN CLUB
433 EAST MAIN STREET
VENTURA, CALIFORNIA

From: *Johnny Cash Fan Club*

P.O. BOX 95, OAK VIEW, CALIFORNIA

Return Postage Guaranteed

TO: *Johnny*

Charles B.
327 S. Laure
Richmond 20,

PRINTED MATTER ONLY

ANTIGUA &
BARBUDA

JOHNNY CASH   75¢

JOHNNY CASH INC.

PERSONAL
DIRECTION
SAUL HOLIFF

HEAD OFFICE

433 E. MAIN ST.
VENTURA, CALIFORNIA
PHONE MILLER 3-0446

CANADIAN
OFFICE

68 KING ST.
LONDON, ONTARIO
PHONE GENERAL 4-377

SPECIAL NEWS BULLETIN FROM THE OFFICE OF *Johnny Cash*

I WALK THE LINE
DON'T TAKE
YOUR GUNS TO TOWN
TENNESSEE FLAT-TOP BOX
THE REBEL—JOHNNY YUMA
BALLAD OF A
TEEN-AGE QUEEN

This large print is a copy of the cover art from the Highwaymen's first album. Johnny showed it to me and asked,
"How would you like me to sign it?" I suggested that he write the opening line to the album's title song. Johnny said, "That's Willie's line.
But let me write my first line, and we'll go to the other guys and I'll ask them to write theirs." Johnny took me to Willie Nelson,
Kris Kristofferson and Waylon Jennings, and each graciously added his first line and signature to the picture.

the Venture nor any Venturer or former Venturer shall thereafter have the right to use the Name for any purpose.

IN WITNESS WHEREOF, the parties hereunto have executed this agreement as of the day and year first written above.

"VENTURERS"

WGJ PRODUCTIONS, INC.

TRACY CONCERTS, INC.

By _____
an authorized signatory

an authorized signatory
c/o Paul, Hastings,
Janofsky & Walker
1299 Ocean Avenue, 5th Floor
Santa Monica, CA 90401
Attn: Gerald A. Margolis, Esq.

Malibu, California 90265

_____
WILLIE NELSON
c/o MARK ROTHBAUM & ASSOCIATES
36 Mill Plain Road, Suite 406
Danbury, Connecticut 06811

_____
JOHNNY CASH
P.O. Box 503
Hendersonville, Tennessee
37075

I have read this Highwaymen Joint Venture Agreement and agree to be bound by its terms and conditions as they relate to my services as Manager.

_____
MARK ROTHBAUM
36 Mill Plain Road
Suite 406
Danbury, Connecticut 0

ENT:00105018.AGR

Following the success of their debut album, Highwayman, Johnny, Willie, Kris and Waylon embarked on their first concert tour in March 1990. The first show drew 56,000 to the Astrodome, the largest crowd to attend an event at the Houston Livestock Show and Rodeo that year. The group continued to tour through 1995. The legal document shown above detailed the Highwaymen's financial and working arrangements.

On February 27, 1993, at a Johnny Cash show in Santa Ana, California, a guy with a long, black beard and wearing dark sunglasses came backstage to meet Johnny. That man was Rick Rubin and ten months later the first fruit of their collaboration was unveiled in a private show at the Viper Room in Los Angeles. Part of the audience included the people pictured on the opposite page: (top) Jeff Lynne, Tom Petty, Johnny and Rubin; (bottom) Johnny Depp and Kate Moss pose with Johnny and June. A clearly nervous and excited Depp practically stuttered the introduction: "Ladies and gentlemen, I can't believe I get to say this: Johnny Cash!" The curtain rose, and there sat Johnny on a stool, surrounded by several acoustic guitars on stands. "This is the first time I've ever done this," he said, "and I'm scared to death." He proceeded to do what he always did: take over the room. He performed "Drive On," which was included on his first album for Rubin, *American Recordings*, in 1994.

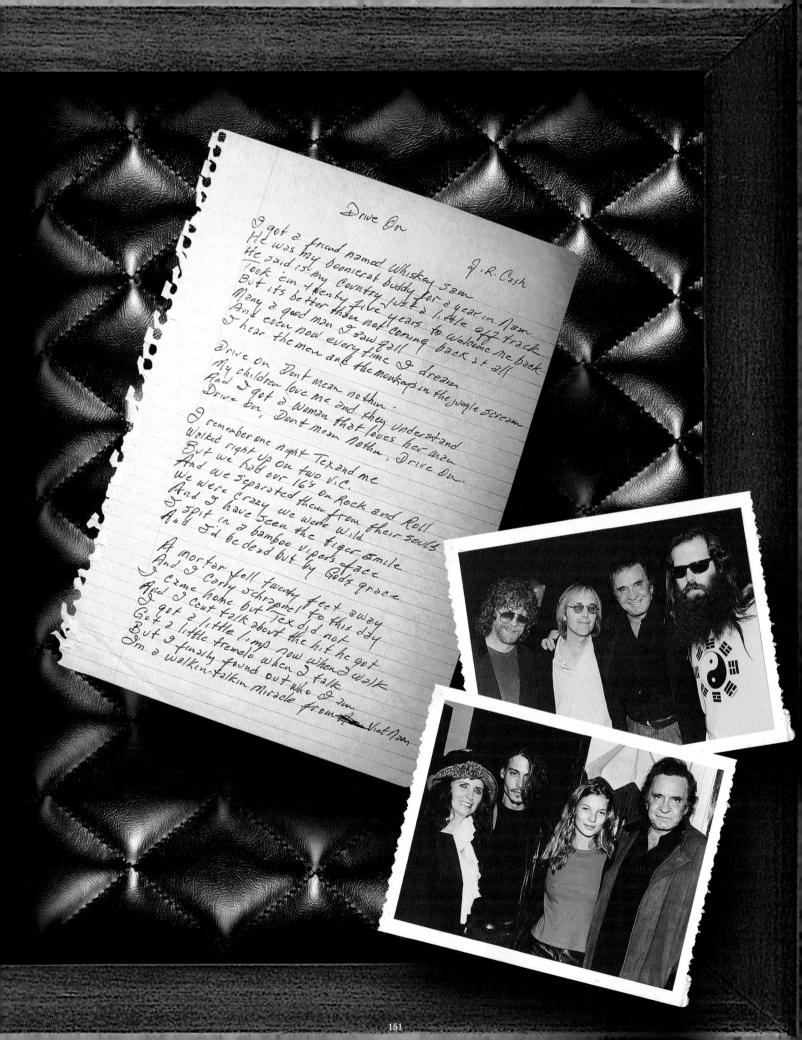

Drive On

J.R. Cash

I got a friend named Whiskey Sam
He was my boonierat buddy for a year in Nam
He said is my country just a little off track
Took 'em twenty five years to welcome me back
But its better than not coming back at all
Many a good man I saw fall
And even now every time I dream
I hear the men and the monkeys in the jungle scream

Drive on   Dont mean nothin
My children love me and they understand
And I got a woman that loves her man
Drive on, Dont mean nothin, Drive on.

I remember one night Tex and me
Walked right up on two V.C.
And we separated them from their souls
But we had our 16's on Rock and Roll
We were crazy we were wild
And I have seen the tiger smile
I spit in a bamboo vipers face
And I'd be dead but by Gods grace

A mortar fell twenty feet away
And I carry schrapnel to this day
I came home but Tex did not
And I cant talk about the hit he got
Got a little limp now when I walk
Got a little tremelo when I talk
But I finally found out who I am
I'm a walkin-talkin Miracle from Viet Nam

CASH

This promotional poster signed by Johnny was for *Unchained*, his second album for the American Recordings label. Tom Petty and the Heartbreakers was Johnny's backup band on the album.

JOHNNY CASH
The Best of COUNTRY

New Recordings

JOHNNY CASH
The BEST of STANDARDS

New Recordings

JOHNNY CASH
The BEST of Gospel

New Recordings

JOHNNY CASH
The BEST of COUNTRY Rock

New Recordings

JOHNNY CASH
The BEST of Traditional

New Recordings

JOHNNY CASH
The BEST of ~~Country~~ LOVE Songs

New Recordings

As Johnny got older, he had a growing interest in organizing his work thematically. He initially wanted to produce a set of six CDs, as depicted in this sketch, featuring his new recordings of standards from various genres. That plan never came to fruition, but Johnny did pick the songs for the three-CD set, *Love, God, Murder*, issued in 2000. The collection spanned Johnny's career and ranged from the obscure to the best known of his songs. During his final years, he often said he wanted to do an album of classic gospel songs, but none of his record companies were interested. His affection for gospel music provided bookends for his career. Sun Records founder Sam Phillips resisted Johnny's desire to be a gospel singer in the 1950s, and 50 years later, Johnny still wanted to do that.

In the mid-1960s, Johnny hired country musicians for shows that he produced. This poster was for an event at KRNT Theater in Des Moines, Iowa. Johnny shared the bill with his future wife, June Carter, and Tex Ritter, one of his childhood heroes. Few of these posters remain; they were usually nailed to poles and placed in store windows, and discarded after the event.

CASH
AMERICAN IV: THE MAN COMES AROUND

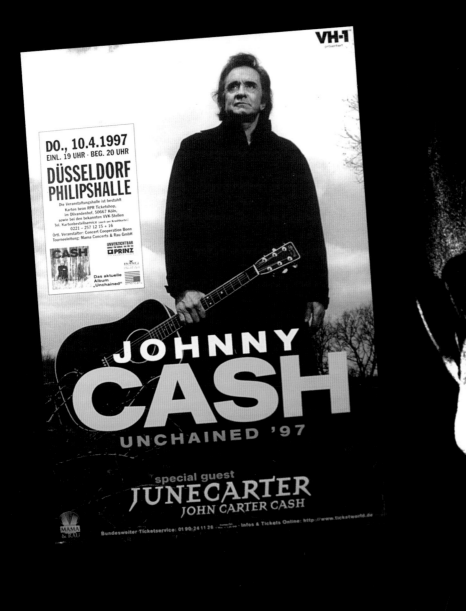

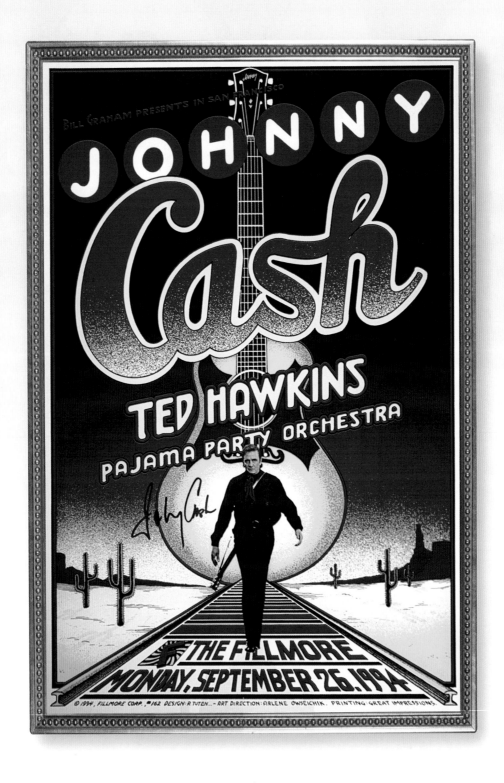

This poster promoted Johnny's 1994 appearance at the renowned Fillmore in San Francisco. The Fillmore has a long and rich history for playing host to classic and cutting-edge rock 'n' roll acts. With the success of Johnny's *American Recordings* album, young crowds packed places like the Fillmore to see him perform. Randy Tuten created the artwork for this poster. He produced many psychedelic posters for Fillmore shows that are highly valued by collectors.

King of the Hill

If you're gong to be
remembered to be the king of the hill
John left his job at the cotton mill
~~Left it~~ in the Harlon mines
one out at quittin time →
Already workin
~~first one in~~ when the whistle blew
They'll complain about a job to do
When they asked ~~who could~~ ~~to be~~ say ou will
~~~~ to be the king of the hill
If you're going you'll
Someday you'll   Go
On Saturday night ~~he went~~ to Harlon town
Shoot some pool and to fool around
Watch the girls and drink bootleg
~~Give~~ to those who borrow and beg
you'd starve to death before you beg
can take no lip from any man
Watch their feet and watch their hands
+ there may be times you'll have to kill
+ if you're gonna be king of the hill
You trade at the commissary store
things may cost you a little bit more
But you keep your job and you stay in line
With the man ~~who~~ owns the Harlon mines
~~that~~

~~Don't mess around~~ ~~to~~ ~~not-~~
~~Give your word and make it~~ ~~Taked~~

When the last time is out of everyt
~~Back the coal~~ ~~is gone~~ on the north bank
Come out in the sun and if you're standing

603 RED RIVER/AUSTIN, TEXAS

This limited edition print commemorated Johnny's appearance at Emo's, a club in Austin, Texas, during the South by Southwest music conference on March 17, 1994. Johnny delivered the keynote address at the conference and performed later that evening at Emo's, a grungy, partly open-air club, for about 500 people. Hundreds of fans were turned away at the door. The mayor of Austin proclaimed it Johnny Cash Day and presented Johnny with a key to the city.

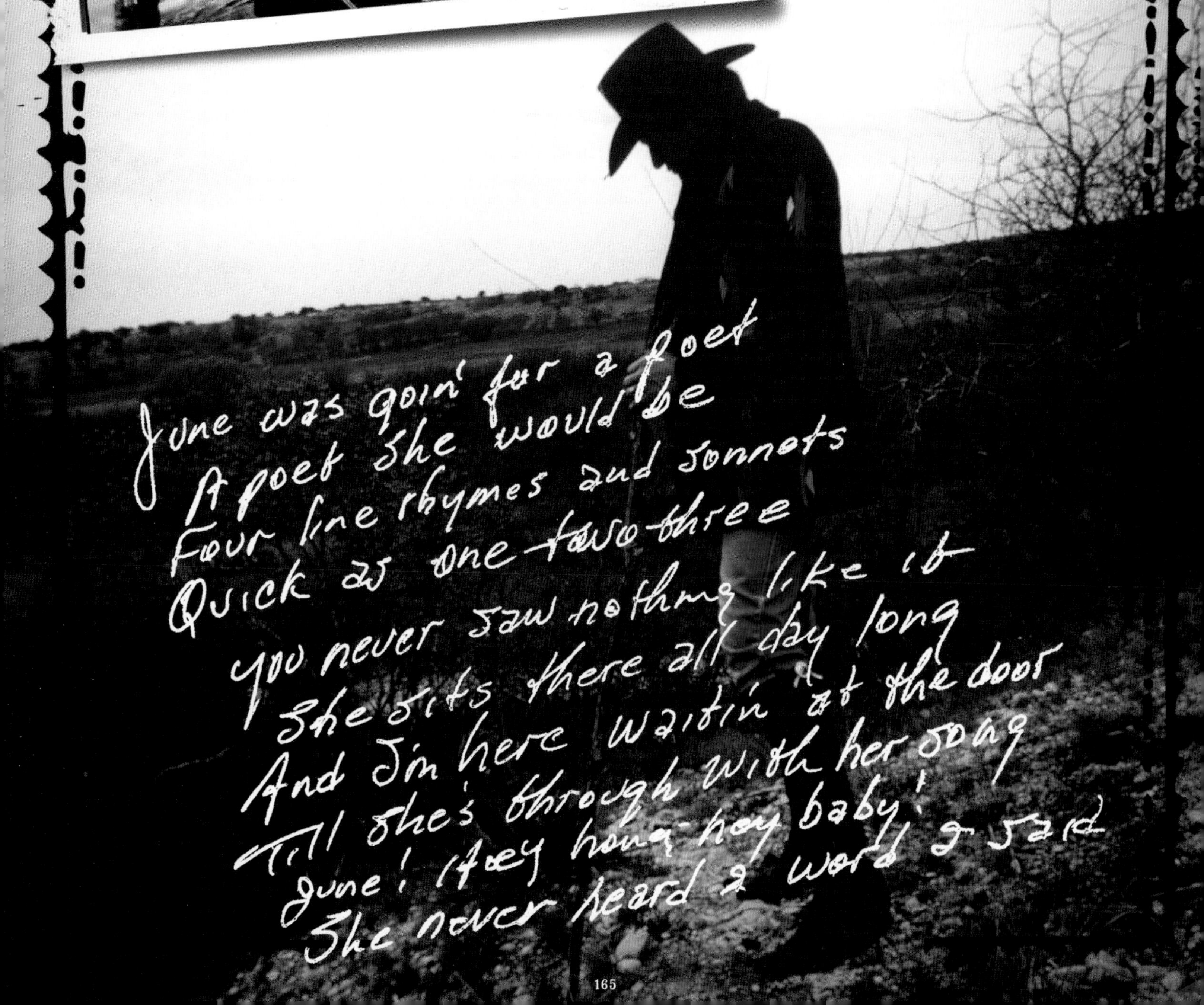

June was goin' for a poet
A poet she would be
Four line rhymes and sonnets
Quick as one-two-three
You never saw nothing like it
She sits there all day long
And I'm here waitin' at the door
Till she's through with her song
June! Hey honey-hey baby!
She never heard a word I said

In 1974, when I was 14, I went to Nashville, Tennessee, to attend Fan Fair, an annual event for fan clubs. On that
trip, I found this little Johnny and June knickknack. It seemed tacky to me, but it was the first three-dimensional
collectible of Johnny that I had seen. I bought it from an older couple who had made figurines of other country stars
as well. I don't remember what it cost, but I am certain it was a huge sum for me at the time. I never really noticed
the inscription on the piece until after both Johnny and June had passed away. Now, every time I look at those
words, "The roses will bloom again," my appreciation for this little piece grows.

I'll say it's true

I've never been in prison
I ~~never~~ don't ever ride a train — my favorite food... octopus
My favorite food aint chicken   I had
And I've never been to plains   it once
I love bright and flashy colors   in spain
Especially red and blue
But if they ask me if it true,
that I still love you, I'll say it's true

I like Okie from Muskogee
I like Welfare Cadillac
Should they come to you please tell em
~~that~~ I don't know why I wear black
I love New York City
Bet your cowboy boots, I do
And if they ask me if it's true
that I still love you, I'll say it true

    yes I'll say
~~I is true too~~ it's true
~~~~
Let ~~em~~ Just don't let it bother you star
But I the old tales all ~~stay~~ twisted
I will set em straight on you

I have not been in the Army
I quit coughing years ago
When they ask if I know Waylon
I will tell them I think so.
And I plan to keep on traveling
For ~~2 hundred years~~ or two
But ~~that~~ if they ask me if it's true
that I still love ya, I'll say its tru

    I will say I don't think so.

LOVE   Cinnamon Hill, Jamaica.
Page 1

Robert Browning said, upon the death of Elizabeth Barrett Browning, "This I believe. Of this I am certain; From this life I shall pass to another better where that lady lives of ~~which~~ whom my very soul is enamoured."

Elizabeth, when living had said to Robert, "How much do I love thee? Let me count the ways."

What has happened to our love language? We have brought it down to ~~three~~ - minute

Page 2

Sound bites - sandwiches in cute words that rhyme. And it's a shame that those love songs are played everywhere with no follow-up kisses to seal the words.

And speaking of sandwiches, June just walked up to me and asked, "John, what would you like for lunch?" She looked right at me with a kind loving look. She might or might not know I was quoting Robert and Elizabeth Browning.

Page 3.

I remember when I fell into June's "Ring of Fire." There was a lot of showing it as well as saying it. Never has there been a deeper love than my love for her. At times it was painful, but we shared the pain so it was just half painful.

Now, even though it mellowed out, the flame of our love still burns. And it burns, burns, burns.

Johnny Cash

And to Job, God
shakes the earth

God maintains
He said to

"IN LIEU OF DONATIONS,
SEND FLOWERS.
I WANT MY BABY TO HAVE
A LOT OF FLOWERS."

JOHNNY CASH

Johnny wanted June to have a big send off and he encouraged friends and fans to send flowers for her funeral service. In fact, he said, "In lieu of donations, send flowers. I want my baby to have a lot of flowers." I have never seen as many flower arrangements as I did at June's service. So many, in fact, that flowers overflowed into every hallway, parlor, Chapel and crevice in the Hendersonville Memorial Gardens Funeral Home. Johnny wrote the poem on page 174 shortly after June's passing.

I threw out all the flowers
that were dead.
I laid the living ones
down by your head
If you could see me
you would laugh I know
For acting like a kid
at 47-0.

But I love you in
death as in life

MY LORD HAS GONE

BY JOHN R. CASH

My Lord has gone
To make a place for me
(To make a place for me)
I heard that it's a mansion
That will stand eternally

I dreamed that I was walking
By the Sea of Galilee
(By the Sea of Galilee)
Thru tear-filled eyes He saw me
And He said follow me
Walking by the Sea of Galilee

I saw Him on the road to Jericho
(I saw Him on the road to Jericho)
He picked up a broken man
And said "I've healed you, go."
Walking on the road to Jericho

They laid the palms before Him
On the way
(On the way)
But there they crucified Him
He'd not a word to say
They treated Him in hatred
On that day

But He called down from Heaven
Just for me
(Just for me)
He said your mansion's ready
As soon you will be
He called down from Heaven just for me.

David "Ferg" Ferguson, Johnny's sound engineer, recorded Johnny for the final time in August 2003 in a session for Johnny's fifth American Recordings album. Johnny had brought with him the lyrics he had written for a new song, "My Lord Has Gone." (As you read the words, it seems obvious that Johnny knew his death was near.) The session was about to end, and Ferg asked Johnny if he wanted to record the new song, but Johnny hadn't composed a melody. He tossed the lyrics on a table as he walked toward the door and said, "You can have them." Johnny died several weeks later. When my wife and I went to Nashville, Tennessee, for Johnny's public memorial service, we arranged a meeting with Ferg at the café in our hotel. As we were led to a table, I noticed that the sheet music of various country songs was reproduced on the place mats. When we got to our table and settled into our seats, each of us had a place mat that bore the words and music to "Folsom Prison Blues." It was an eerie coincidence, but I truly felt that Johnny was among us. Ferg pulled out an envelope and presented me with one of the best gifts I have ever received: Johnny's handwritten lyrics for his last song. (The sheet is reproduced on the following page.) "I know John would want you to have these," Ferg said.

My Lord Has Gone

My Lord has gone
To make a place for me
I heard that it's a mansion
That will stand eternally

I dreamed that I was walking
By the Sea of Galilee
Thru tear-filled eyes he saw me
And he said follow me
Walking by the Sea of Galilee

I saw Him on the road to Jericho
He picked up a broken man
And said "I've healed you too"
Walking on the road to Jericho

They laid the palms before Him
On the Way

But then they crucified Him
He'd not a word to say
They treated Him in hatred
On that day

But He called down from Heaven
Just for me

He said your mansion's ready
As you soon will be
He called down from Heaven just for me